Horseback Schoolmarm

Margot and Orphan Annie, Margot's mare during her schoolmarm years and for nineteen years thereafter. (Photo by Robert Pringle, at Soldier Creek Ranch, 1952.)

Horseback Schoolmarm

Montana, 1953–1954

Margot Liberty

UNIVERSITY OF OKLAHOMA PRESS : NORMAN

Also by Margot Liberty
(ed.) *American Indian Intellectuals* (St. Paul, Minn., 1978)
(and W. Raymond Wood, eds.) *Anthropology on the Great Plains* (Lincoln, Neb., 1980)
(and Barry Head) *Working Cowboy: Recollections of Ray Holmes* (Norman, Okla., 1995)
(and John Stands In Timber) *Cheyenne Memories* (New Haven, Conn., 1967;
2nd ed., 1998)
(ed.) *American Indian Intellectuals of the Nineteenth and Early Twentieth Centuries*
(Norman, Okla., 2002)
(ed.) *A Northern Cheyenne Album* (Norman, Okla., 2006)
(and John Stands In Timber) *A Cheyenne Voice: The Complete
John Stands In Timber Interviews* (Norman, Okla., 2013)

The poems "Schoolmarm," "Summer School 1953, Ithaca," "Nocturne," and
"Twilight" are reprinted from *Songs and Snippets: Poems by Margot Liberty* (n.p.:
Xlibris, 2010).

Library of Congress Cataloging-in-Publication Data
Names: Liberty, Margot, author.
Title: Horseback schoolmarm : Montana, 1953–1954 / Margot Liberty.
Description: Norman : University of Oklahoma Press, 2016. | Includes
   bibliographical references.
Identifiers: LCCN 2015046964 | ISBN 978-0-8061-5388-9 (hardcover) ISBN
978-0-8061-9002-0 (paper) Subjects: LCSH: Liberty, Margot. | Teachers—
Montana—Custer County—
   Biography. | Rural schools—Montana—Custer County—History—20th
   century. | Education, Rural—Montana—Custer County—History—
   20th century.
Classification: LCC LA2317.L578 A3 2016 | DDC 371.10092—dc23
LC record available at http://lccn.loc.gov/2015046964

To Paula and Henry Liberty,
in spite of it all

and to the memory of
Ellen Emerson Cotton
of Four Mile Ranch, Decker, Montana

Schoolmarm

Lunch pails and overshoes
Two small figures trudging home
Through February mud.

Waving back once at the teacher standing
Broom in hand, at the schoolhouse door

"You look like ducks!" she calls.
"Puddle ducks! Good night!"
And so they turn
To walk the puddle-jeweled two miles home

Broom in hand at the schoolhouse door
Waving once more at the little boys leaving.

Lunch boxes and overshoes,
Two small figures sloshing bravely home,
First-graders,
Two miles through puddled February mud.

Contents

List of Illustrations

Figures

Map

Preface

The SH School—Before and After

Some readers will wonder how I wound up teaching an isolated, one-room country school in southeastern Montana just after graduating from Cornell University in New York State in 1953. I had grown up in New York City and Washington, D.C., the daughter of two distinguished writers.[1] My family spent four summers on dude and cattle ranches in the Sheridan, Wyoming, area before the outbreak of World War II. And, just after the bombing of Pearl Harbor, when my mother chose to winter in Wyoming in 1941–42, I rode horseback myself to a one-room country school, the Beckton School. We could not go west during the remaining years of the war, but I maintained a passionate love of horses while riding at stables in Maryland and Virginia with a group of girls known as the Junior Cavalry and my precious Virginia friend Louise Laylin. During my final two high school years at the Madeira School in Greenway, Virginia, during 1947 and 1948, I won first team horsemanship (there were five teams, the first two providing fox hunting and show jumping), which was my lifelong proudest achievement. We had never had enough money for me to have a horse of my own, but I saved up, and on the way west with my mother in 1951, we stopped at a livestock sale. It was there I bought for $30 the gray filly I named Orphan Annie, who had been destined for the dog food market as ranchers then did not usually retain fillies as saddle stock. For more than twenty years, Orphan Annie would play a major role in my life. She was almost human, as sweet-tempered and sensitive as an animal can ever be.

In 1949 I went to the College of Agriculture at Cornell University and graduated with a Bachelor of Science degree in 1953. My college summers were spent in Wyoming and Montana, where my mother was engaged in many writing ventures. I had jobs on ranches in Sheridan and in Birney, Montana, on the Tongue River, where I was to spend many subsequent years. In 1952 I became romantically involved with a Birney ranch hand (or cowboy), and by fall our attachment was approaching the serious stage. When I graduated from Cornell in 1953, I needed to know what future this relationship might entail, so I decided to try for a job as a country schoolteacher to find out, among other things, if I could stand the harsh winters and isolation in the Far West. First, though, I needed a teaching certificate.

At Cornell University in my day there was a prevailing opinion that courses in education were a waste of time. Students of four-year programs in liberal arts, the sciences, or agriculture were thought to have acquired sufficient knowledge in various subjects to be able to teach in elementary schools. All they needed was a modicum of teacher training gained in a short course that encompassed the main points of technique and method. Thus, Cornell had introduced a six-week summer course in education for graduates with bachelor's degrees, after which the State of New York issued an elementary certificate with the assumption that further course work could follow as needed. The director of our Cornell program during this time was named Loretta Klee. Dr. Klee was a wonderful teacher and mentor to all students. I kept in touch with her from the wilds of Montana during that entire first year I spent teaching in the one-room school on the SH Ranch.

During my accelerated summer-school session at the Cornell University College of Education I was able to get a private study carrel in the main library on campus. In this tall and majestic building, one could keep one's books together for an extended period, which was a huge convenience, and peer down from a high window on the summer-school student pedestrians below. My great discovery that summer was the book *My Country School Diary*, written by a grade-school teacher named Julia Weber, who taught more than forty students in eight grades somewhere in upstate New York. Her directions as to how to manage such a situation, including lunchtime and recess, were marvels of inspiration and humor. I felt her presence at my side throughout the following year.

But on hot summer days in the library when I was longing for the green breezy pastures of the MacMillan farm where I was living with a family and their horses a few miles west of campus, rebellion occasionally struck, and one day a poem came forth:

Summer School 1953, Ithaca

My arms have grown warm in the sun and my hair is a
  mess,
And I will not come down off my tower into virtuousness.

For all you who chatter and cheep and go by on the walk
Like a band of ridiculous sheep making sensible talk,

But sit here and soak in the sun, feeling evil and free,
Rejoicing in all the somnambulant sinnings in me.

The SH School had been moved to its location site sixty miles south of
Miles City two or three years before I arrived there. The owner of the
SH Ranch, a Miles City businessman named Ed Love, wanted to retain
his hired hands when their children reached compulsory school age,
so he bought a vacant schoolhouse and moved it to the ranch. Even
then it was difficult to find teachers to live in such remote and primitive circumstances, so at the last minute the school board snapped me
up, with my Cornell certificate.

The school was also sixty miles south of the 4D Ranch at Birney,
where my boyfriend was employed. It was a long, one-way commute,
so I was not able to see much of him. I had to live alone in a "teacherage," walled off at one end of the schoolroom. It had electricity but
no phone, plumbing, or running water. The nearest house was more
than a mile away, and my car had to be parked even farther away across
the river, to be reached by a swinging cable-car device known as a Go
Devil. I kept my saddle horse Orphan Annie in the schoolyard.

All went well until it began to get cold, and I had much trouble
running the coal stove in the schoolroom, the only source of heat
for me and my students. Luckily I did not have to manage all this by
myself. I was befriended by a second cowboy, Forrest Liberty, who
had been hired to work at the SH. He built a shed for Orphan Annie
before cold weather hit in late fall and taught me to bank a coal stove.
As I have written elsewhere, proximity won the day. We were married
in 1955 and stayed together for seven years. We had two children

before it became clear that this boat was not going to float.

After my year at the SH, I was hired as an elementary school teacher on the Northern Cheyenne Reservation on Tongue River near Birney. I remained at this government day school for four years, becoming steeped in Northern Cheyenne tradition and ultimately writing *Cheyenne Memories* with John Stands in Timber, the seventy-five-year-old historian of the tribe.[2] I wrote the "Schoolmarm" manuscript after my first year at the Birney Day School. As federal employees, school staff members were required to stay on site throughout the year, the staff consisting of myself and the Cheyenne cook, Mary Wolftooth Sand Crane. We were supposed to spend our time cleaning and polishing floors, but I stole enough hours to complete "Schoolmarm" during summer 1954. It was never submitted for publication and was "lost" in my files for sixty years.

During two later summers (1961 and 1962), I worked as a ranger-historian at what was then called the Custer Battlefield National Monument (now the Little Big Horn Battlefield National Monument), by then with my two small children. During one of those summers, I met Adamson Hoebel, a famous anthropologist and chair of the Department of Anthropology at the University of Minnesota. Professor Hoebel offered me a graduate fellowship at Minnesota, where I did five years of graduate work toward a Ph.D. in anthropology, completed in 1973. Then came many years of research, writing, and teaching on three graduate anthropology faculties (at the universities of Nebraska, Missouri, and Pittsburgh), along with a fellowship at the Smithsonian Institution under the direction of John C. Ewers. Later I did filmmaking and museum work, and organized two national conferences, each of which resulted in a published book.[3]

Since 1981, I have lived in Sheridan, Wyoming, where I have written two contributions to the Smithsonian *Handbook of North American Indians*, focusing on the Cheyenne and Omaha Indians respectively; and have worked on the documentary *On the Cowboy Trail*, concerning modern cattle ranching, which aired nationally as part of the PBS Odyssey series in 1981. I have published additional books, including *A Northern Cheyenne Album* (2006), with photographs by Thomas B. Marquis and commentary by John Woodenlegs, and *A Cheyenne Voice:*

The Complete Stands In Timber Interviews (2013). I have also worked in photography, and "Ranching on Tongue River," an exhibition of my photographs, was presented at the Bradford Brinton Memorial at Big Horn, Wyoming, in 2010. A book by the same title is in the works for the University of Oklahoma Press. But this book has come first.

This memoir provides a glimpse back in time to rural Montana in the mid-1950s and reflects my thoughts and experiences during my year as a horseback schoolmarm. It has been lightly edited for clarity and consistency but otherwise appears here as I first wrote it in 1955. Note that the narrative, written in 1953, occasionally evinces the biases and prejudices of its time—regarding rural versus urban cultures, Indians versus whites, stereotypically "good" people versus "bad"— rather than more modern notions. As such, this is a document of its time, no different from other memoirs written during an earlier era.

Acknowledgments

After having vanished into the oblivion of my personal storage, the manuscript for the present book turned up in 2014, more than half a century after I first wrote it. There it was, typewritten on colored sheets, bound up with a length of string. I had completely forgotten about it. I called Byron Price, director of the University of Oklahoma Press, and said, "I have found this lost manuscript describing my year in an isolated one-room Montana schoolhouse half a century ago, in 1953–54, when I was just out of college." He responded with his famous dictum, "Send It To Me."

I am thankful to Byron for seeing the value in this somewhat funky little old manuscript. I am thankful to Charles E. Rankin, associate director and editor-in-chief at OU Press, for enjoying the material and for sending it on the readers who supported its publication. And I am thankful to Alice Stanton, who saw the material through the editorial process, so that you may now hold it in your hands.

I am indebted to others as well:

To my father, Pulitzer Prize winner Henry F. Pringle, who said that to write a book, the prescription was simple: "Place the seat of the pants in the seat of the chair."

To my mother, Helena Huntington Smith, whose three brilliant books of western history created a difficult trail to follow, and whose passion for the American West contributed to so much of the adventure and the heartaches as well as achievements of my own professional life.

To my father's second wife, Katherine Douglas Pringle, whose grace, intellect, and elegance, and whose generous love for another woman's children, meant very much to them in their maturing years.

To my brother Robert M. Pringle for the photographs of Annie and me.

To research assistants Winifred Galloway and Marilyn Leander of

Sheridan, Wyoming, and to Judy Slack, Wyoming Room, Sheridan County Fulmer Public Library.

To counselors Don Boone, MSW, LCSW; Linda S. Rice, EdD, LAT; and Beth V. Kelsey, EdD, LPC.

And to Caroline Yellowtail Houston, and to Donna Shelley, of Sheridan, Wyoming.

Horseback Schoolmarm

Margot riding Orphan Annie.
(Photo by Robert Pringle, at Soldier Creek Ranch, 1952.)

Prologue

Crossing the sagebrush-speckled wastes of our western states, the traveler will see more than once, whether from railroad tracks or highway, a small, square, white building whose sheer loneliness will proclaim it as a school. It looks so tiny somehow—such a solitary pinpoint of civilization in so vast a stretch of untrammeled space. This traveler may smile, perhaps remembering parents' or grandparents' tales of hickory-armed teachers, of privies and potbellied stoves, and of long on-foot or horseback journeys to school in winter across snow-driven winter miles. And the traveler may wonder in passing how much time has gone by since this little schoolhouse rattled to the tramp of children's boots or calmed to the ringing of a recess bell.

It may have happened more recently than he might think—maybe last year, maybe today. In Montana in 1953 more than nine hundred such one-room schools continued in session each winter, in districts so remote and thinly settled that consolidation seemed impossible. Here, things of the past both good and bad move close to one. There is the poor heat, the absence of plumbing, the miles of terrible roads. There are children few in number and varied in age, demanding much of their harried teacher, who must divide her time fairly among all. And often the equipment and books fall far below the standards that prevail in town.[1]

Yet notice the frantic town administrator trying to drum up interest in the PTA, and then look in at the country school while a group of mothers busily polish and scrub, getting ready for a community dance. Notice the expensive town playground equipment getting smashed and initial-scarred, and then watch the country kids helping their fathers dig postholes for a homemade set of swings. It is the same the world over: what one has had a hand in building, one will not want to tear down. And the country people today must still build for themselves; nobody else will do it for them.

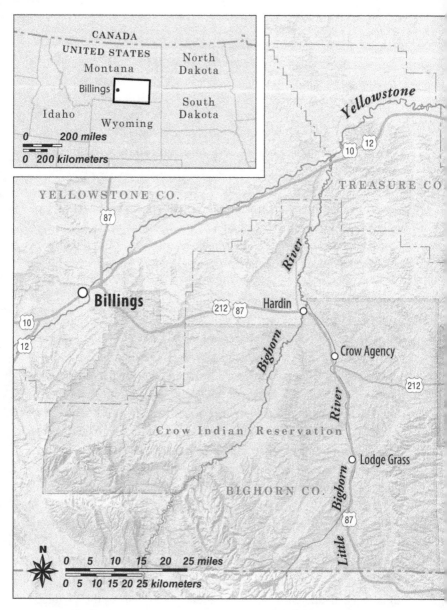

Region of southeastern Montana where Margot Liberty taught school, including locations of the SH School and the Garland School. (Map by Ben Pease. Copyright © 2016, University of Oklahoma Press.)

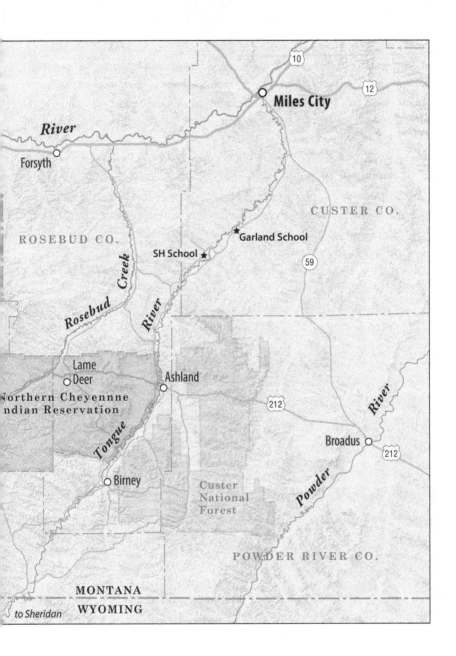

This is the story of a year spent at one country school and of what happened when its seven children came in contact with a recently graduated, inexperienced teacher from back East who knew little about teaching school and even less about living by herself in a "teacherage" a mile from the closest neighbor and sixty miles from the nearest town: Miles City, Montana.

It tells of the seven children she came to know, children who found new strength when they were clearly seen as individuals, an insight made elusive for teachers in more crowded schools, but still, in our case, possible. And it speaks of the far-flung spaces of Montana and the ways of life that battle one another for possession of the land.

It is a touch of the past in the present. The modern rush for efficiency, for mass production in all phases of life, has not managed to affect a land where people are so few and space is so tremendous. One depends on oneself to a great extent, when at night the nearest humanity is reduced to a twinkle of lights no brighter than that of the nearest star. And the values of an older way of life stand out well, when the people of a community seize any excuse for long social get-togethers; or when you find yourself alone with a broken leg, as I did, knowing beyond any shadow of a doubt that when you need him, your neighbor will be there.

CHAPTER ONE

Here Comes the Schoolmarm

I learned some details about the SH School before I was ever confronted with the reality of living there. I had already determined that I wanted a job as a country schoolteacher out west. After I sent in an application for an open position at the SH School in Montana, I received a response from the school clerk, which arrived while I was still living in Ithaca, New York. His letter read as follows:

Dear Miss Pringle,

Thank you for your application. We do not have a teacher for our school yet but your qualifications sound adequate, so perhaps we can assume that we have one now. There will be four children in Grade One, one in Grade Two, one in Grade Three, and one in Grade Seven.

You will have a very nice sized teacherage to live in under the same roof, although the school itself is not extra large. There is a well close to the school house and electricity of which the school district pays up to five or six dollars.

Perhaps you would like to know something of the surroundings. The SH Ranch is a very large ranch about 50 miles from Miles City. There is a good deal of irrigated land and acres and acres of dry land farming. The closest home from the school is about one half mile.

Would you let us know your definite answer as soon as possible.

Yours truly,

Ted Hirsch

P.S. There are a few things in the teacherage in the line of cupboards, but there is no bed or stove. I would suggest a hot plate for light cooking.

I returned a definite answer in the next mail as requested—definitely negative.

It was a curious turn of events that led me to the door of that same school clerk late in the month of August 1953.

I had driven some 1,300 miles back and forth across mostly truly awful Montana roads, hunting for a teaching job. I had dealt in fumbling fashion with three flat tires, rescued in one case by a carload of obliging Crow Indians who changed my shredded tire in a jiffy. They were gallantry itself, fetching their own bumper jack because mine didn't work very well, and conversing in unintelligible Crow the whole time with a gray-pigtailed, sunglasses-adorned old man in their back seat.

Before they drove away we all introduced ourselves. "I'm War Horse," said the younger of the two. "He's Tobacco."

War Horse and Tobacco were about the only accommodating people I would meet for some time afterward. The Indian Service, for which I would have liked to teach, was desperately short of teachers, but it was just as desperately clinging to regulations that classed me as under-qualified. I could probably have the job I wanted, they assured me, in a subnormal or submarginal or sub-something status, but I would have to wait until the day school started before I would know whether I was hired, and of course if anyone better qualified came along after that they would have to fire me. So sorry, please.

Somewhat chastened, I fished out the letters I had treated so haughtily a few months before. The SH School, it turned out, was still teacherless—so I decided to drive out and look at it after all. In town they said you could drive through the river once you got to the ranch—just plunge on in. Apprehensively, I traversed the forty-five miles of gravel road to the ranch and to the edge of the river, which looked mighty full to me for plunging. I then experienced the alarming sensation of driving a car off a sloping bank into a wide swirling river.

Weeks later, in one of our geography books, I found a paragraph that explained condescendingly, "There are places in our country where streams must still be forded due to the lack of bridges." I laughed weakly and pointed it out to my seventh-grader, who failed to see anything humorous in the picture of Indians on ragged ponies, breasting a wide creek.

Having somehow navigated the river, I arrived at the main part

The SH School in 1953. (Author photo)

of the SH Ranch and, meandering through clouds of dust and the quagmire where someone had let an irrigation ditch wander across the road, I found my way to the house of the school clerk. Mr. Hirsch was not at home, busy in the hayfield. His wife, however—an attractive, slender blond woman in her twenties—offered to show me around. We departed in her car, driving up the twisty and rutted mile to the schoolhouse, with her four small youngsters clamoring over the back seat and a thick cloud of dust rolling up behind us importantly— announcing to all the neighbors that Ruthie had the new schoolmarm girl and was taking her up to see the school.

I had expected about what I saw: a square little weather-beaten building, its white paint scaling off; a shed or two; a pair of dilapidated privies; a windmill and a cow tank—all scattered on a treeless flat where the dry hills ended and the irrigated fields began their march toward the river.

We went inside to look around, while the Hirsch kids tumbled and squealed and scribbled all over the green blackboards. A door at one end of the small schoolroom led to the partitioned-off teacherage. I remembered what the letter had said about no stove or bed, but the prospect was still pretty bleak. The room where the sole faculty member had to live was a barren compartment containing only a couple of

9

battered cabinets and a lonely rocking chair. I inspected the rocking chair more closely, while Mrs. Hirsch explained that it was one of the few survivors of the fire that had burned the old ranch house down. Its time-grayed covering was painstakingly embroidered by hand, picturing not flowers, but a blanket-draped and top-hatted Indian. His eyes held a curious leer as he puffed on an ancient peace pipe.

"With Pipe of Peace," read the raveled motto, "All Troubles Cease."

Mrs. Hirsch, in fact, seemed to be offering an apologetic pipe of peace as she stood there. What a place! I thought wistfully of other schools I had seen, and also of the unpleasant alternative of waiting tables all winter in a town restaurant.

That latter possibility swung the balance. In tactful silence, we walked out and shut the door on the inhospitable teacherage. At least this place presented a few challenges, I reasoned to myself. I felt a growing certainty that I was going to work here.

I moved in some days later. Two of the mothers had gone ahead of me to scrub the schoolhouse floor, and children swarmed out to meet me as I drove bumpily into the yard.

"Mama Mama Mama!" they screamed. "Here comes the school-marm! The teacher, Mama! Here comes the teacher! Here comes the schoolmarm!"

Good heavens, I thought to myself. You are. You actually are. A SCHOOLMARM!

I got out of the car gingerly, carrying a bowl of long-suffering gold-fish wrapped in discarded rayon underwear. The two fish had trav-eled more than two hundred miles from Billings, and were rather the worse for wear. Their undignified covering had twice saved them from disaster—once when we lurched over a set of remarkably deep ruts and again when I suddenly had to yield right-of-way to a cow. I felt quite tender toward my little fish. Pioneers, we were—the three of us together. And pioneers they remained to the end, when their water froze in the schoolroom one January evening.

The ring of fascinated children parted as I walked toward the school-house.

"How is the water here?" I asked a small boy with a shock of fine blond hair. "The fish would sure like some fresh water."

"It's okay," he answered cheerily. "The pump works fine; it's a real easy pump. Come, I'll show you."

We all went out to the pump, and the little boy—named Leslie, I learned—demonstrated it manfully.

"Easier than our pump," he puffed, as a torrent of dark brown water rushed out of a length of pipe. "Only she's dirty and rusty now. Papa's got to fix the windmill and pump it all out. It needs a new stick."

I looked up in the direction he pointed, knowing little about windmills or their ailments.

"How does it work?" I asked.

"The wind blows the wheel around, but you got to turn it on," offered a little girl with brown hair and eyes. "Then the wheel pushes on the stick and that pumps the water out."

"Papa's got to fix that stick, all right," said Leslie in tones of foreboding. "Mama's been after him quite a while but he keeps on forgettin' and forgettin' . . ."

"Well," I decided, "I don't think these fish would like that rusty water too well, do you?"

We agreed that the fish had better wait until the water was clearer. Together, we went across the yard into the school—the first of so many times.

Both families were nice about offering me the sofas in their homes as places to sleep until a bed could be borrowed for the teacherage, but a glance into their crowded houses showed that it would be quite a strain to accommodate an extra person. I thanked them and explained that since I had a sleeping bag, I would be all right at the schoolhouse.

I drove back as it was growing dark, and the windows flashed my car lights back as I approached, giving the illusion that the place was full of spooks. Stumbling over last year's half-dissolved ash heap, I carried the sleeping bag up the steps and into the teacherage. Home!

As I unrolled my sleeping bag on the floor, I wondered what I had gotten myself into. Bugs swarmed through the screenless door I had left open to catch the breeze and danced around the overhead lightbulb, throwing weird shadows on the tan, unpainted walls. The windmill emitted an occasional rusty groan, accompanied by the faraway bellowing of a cow. The white porcelain pitcher of water sitting on one cabinet seemed to mock my ignorance of all things unmodernized. When I got up to release the trapped bug that was crashing around inside a tin-lined flour drawer, I found also the decaying remains of a mouse. Two sagging shelves pounded up by last year's teacher— who had been something of a real carpenter—held the assortment of cooking utensils and dishes supplied by the school board. Two or three broken-handled cups sat beside a lidless coffee percolator and a collection of tin cans. There was also a brown-stained bowl with a large crack running from side to side. That was all.

I switched off the light and slid down inside my sleeping bag. "Kiddo," I told myself firmly, "the first step tomorrow will be a trip back to town."

With funds supplied by my parents after a frantic SOS, I went shopping the next day in Miles City, sixty miles away. I bought a bedspread, optimistically counting on a place to put it in the near future. I bought loads of groceries, mostly all dried or canned to eliminate the need for refrigeration, and bolts of bright red cotton for making curtains to cover the nakedly gaping windows and closets and shelves. I think there were twenty yards of the stuff! Next the dime store provided silverware, sharp knives, and a dish pan, a can opener, a potato peeler, a coffee pot, mixing bowls, glasses, salt-and-pepper shakers, and an assortment of cooking ware and dishes decorated with merry cowboys; scrubbing supplies, towel racks, coat hangers, lightbulbs, extension cords, a clothes sprinkler, and, finally, a fat glass lamp with a red shade.

The saleslady looked more and more sympathetic as she wrapped and totaled my enormous purchase.

"Dearie," she finally ventured. "Did you just get married?"

"No," I snapped rather testily. "I am just going to try to teach school."

The car grunted as I stowed away my purchases, but there was more to come. Next stop was the office of the county superintendent of rural schools. A brief survey of my schoolroom had revealed it to be about as well equipped as my own quarters. Fortunately the county office performed the wonderful service of lending textbooks to needy schools, and I was well qualified to apply.

After a pleasant chat with the friendly superintendent, I nearly emptied the shelves in the office. I took every single new book on any subject I could find, especially ones with bright pictures. I also took first-, second-, and third-grade texts in all the usual subjects, and several kinds of each when I could find them. I discovered pristine, shiny samples of workbooks sent to the office by traveling salesmen, and was generously allowed to take a batch of those. I took so much that I had to make eight trips back and forth to the car.

"What shall I do about advising the school board to buy some books of our own?" I asked.

"It's entirely up to the teacher," I was told. "You do all the ordering out of the catalog yourself—the board doesn't know what you need."

"But I'm not at all sure I know myself," I confessed. "I'm kind of new at all this."

"Of course you know, dearie," came the encouraging reply. "Wait a bit to see what the children can use best, and then go ahead and buy it for them."

"Thank you," I said feebly—and departed. One thing I was learning for certain: there was a lot of freedom to this job. At this point I began to wish fervently for a dictatorial superior who would tell me what to do. It dawned on me later that nobody realized how ignorant I was.

I spent the next day or two at the schoolhouse trying to get settled. An all-night siege with a borrowed paintbrush resulted in teacherage walls of a very pleasant sagebrush color, and then the horrified discovery at roughly 3 A.M. that my supply of paint was not going to finish the job. In panic I diluted what was left to half strength, but the paint mercilessly ran out anyhow. A jagged tan patch ran along the top of one wall to merge with a totally tan ceiling.

I had mixed the color myself and there would be no duplicating it. "Well the hell with it," I decided. And tan that ceiling was—and is, doubtless, to this very day.

With the new color, however, the teacherage perked up. I eventually also got my red curtains up on the windows and closet and shelves; my pictures and radio came from the East; and the neighbors finally supplied a bed, which looked elegant under its new plaid spread. An orange crate accommodated itself nicely as a bedside table, covered with extra material chopped off one side of the bedspread. The rocking-chair Indian continued to leer and admonish about pipes of peace, but

I became used to him. When my own boxes of books were hauled from the freight depot, I spread them out on a lengthy shelf constructed of bricks and rough-sawed boards. My quarters felt cozy now, and I was beginning to feel pioneerish. Let the snow fall, let the river rise!

"Hey," said Leslie to his mother in hushed tones when I was at their house one evening. "That teacher's got it fixed *pretty* in there, with *red* stuff and all."

I swelled up with pleasure, deciding Leslie had great potential.

A prettier teacherage did not imply a more convenient one though. The difficulties inherent in cooking any sort of meal on a single hot plate, for instance, soon became apparent. Each dish took quite a while to cook, by which time its predecessors had become cold. A simple supper of soup, hamburger, canned spinach, and coffee became a marathon meal whose preparation lasted well over an hour. I put the soup on to heat and ate it while the hamburger was cooking, then ate the hamburger while the spinach was cooking, then ate the spinach and took a nap while the coffee was coming to a boil, and then drank the coffee while waiting for the dishwater to heat. If I wanted a bath after the dishes were done, some more heating and waiting were involved. I soon learned to heat water and make coffee ahead of time whenever possible. An even simpler solution was to eat things raw.

Thanks to my mother, I had another hot plate within a few weeks—a two-burner one. She was worried that I would be found starving—and frozen to the floor.

Jubilant about being able to cook *three* things at once, I plugged all the burners in—and promptly blew a fuse.

Bathing, too, was a complicated process, as the teacherage lacked any sort of tub. I tried standing in the small tin washbasin and pouring water over myself from the watering can, which was better designed for filling car radiators than for the purpose to which I put it. Invariably after such a bout of cleanliness, the floor turned into a swamp. I began to understand why people used to take baths on Saturday nights only— and brave souls they were.

I washed clothes and hung them to dry on a battered ladder propped up against the school building.

I invented a sort of indoor sun dial by noticing where the shadow of the door sill fell at 7:00, 7:15, and 7:30 P.M. radio time, hoping to rely on this system until my clock arrived, courtesy again of my mother. But the earth disobligingly shifted its position in outer space, rendering my pencil markings useless within three or four days. Oh well, the clock would be here before long.

Subsisting on a meal of soup three times a day, I dissolved into a state of jitters trying to plan for the first day of school. Such virginal experiences are said to hold terrors for graduates of four-year teachers' colleges, trained to the teeth, who must tackle no more than a single grade. With no more than six weeks of teacher training to fall back on, I was going to have to teach at least ten subjects on four different grade levels, assuming that all the children in each grade were working at the same speed, which none of them ever did. However, three of my grades had only one child apiece. One-room schoolhouses have their compensations.

I spent many midnight vigils boning through the telephone-book-size course of studies supplied by the State of Montana, trying to memorize the forty or more separate standards with which I was supposed to be familiar—first grade arithmetic, second-grade arithmetic, third-grade arithmetic, seventh-grade arithmetic; first-grade reading, second-grade reading, third-grade reading, seventh-grade reading—and so on. I never did memorize the guidelines. It seemed that one's horse sense had best be one's guide, at least for the first few weeks.

Even after you had a rough idea of the standards, there was still the business of how to keep a school operating on four different grade levels—galloping from one grade to the next, setting one student to work on his own, while teaching the second, and referring the third to a set of printed directions on the blackboard, while the fourth cuts out pictures and the fifth is God knows where doing God knows what. It was fortunate there were just four, not eight.

I had set aside the day before school opened for final planning, according to a schedule I had worked out earlier. Despite my days of preparation, when I actually sat down to ordain what my four grades of children were each to be doing at all moments of the day, I nearly dissolved into panic. I made my plans in a state of hysteria, and time rushed by. At noon I had the day of the seventh-grader done—and that was all. I was thoroughly mixed up as to which pages he was to be reading in what books, and finally assigned him a lengthy composition in the despairing hope that the exercise would last him at least halfway through the afternoon. Then I struck on a rich idea. During arithmetic period he could compute how many square feet there were in the walls and ceiling of the classroom, with a future view to painting them; and would he please measure all dimensions accurately, subtracting from the total the area taken up by three blackboards and four windows?

So much for Gene, I thought bitterly. *That* ought to hold him a while.

On the blackboard I chalked up a determined WELCOME TO SCHOOL, listing underneath it EDDIE * LESLIE * GARY * DICK * PANSY * BILLY * GENE in various artistic tints. Then I returned to my splintered desk. The desks were lined up about as well as I could manage, in four short rows; my laboriously constructed bulletin board was covered with big bright pictures; the science table adorned with goldfish and a box of seashells; and art materials laid out on back desks not actually used by the children. I would keep the younger children busy with art projects part of the time, and the second- and third-graders could read to me, and what about lunch pails? Leave them on the porch, I guessed, and show the beginners where the toilets were, and tell them all to call me Miss Margot because I wasn't old enough or mean enough to be Miss Pringle yet. Not yet.

I tore some pages out of old workbooks for the children to use in arithmetic and resolutely turned my eyes away from the cupboard that was bulging with an accumulation of materials dating back fifty years. Then I found some calendar pages to use in the first-grade number-finding; dug out a stack of pictures I had brought from the East, placing them in an accessible spot in the classroom; and hopefully searched for a lively story to read after lunch, finding nothing that the younger ones could possibly understand. To fill that slot I decided on a trip around the schoolyard to inventory our meager possessions, and pinned up a measuring tape to take pupil heights with—jumping with alarm when it fell down again.

"Heavens," I exclaimed to myself. "You *are* nervous."

At five o'clock that afternoon I was in a state of numb shock. Luckily it was fifty miles to the nearest bar. I gulped coffee for a while, puttering around nervously, and finally went to bed secure in the knowledge of one thing: that never, never, never in the history of Montana had a more inadequately prepared young woman approached her first teaching day.

Here comes the schoolmarm, I thought sarcastically. Schoolmarm, indeed!

CHAPTER TWO

A Full First Day

I paced nervously back and forth among the assemblage of seven pupils and their parents. They were standing in awkward clusters, waiting for the dreadful moment of launching when the little shipful of children and teacher would be left on its own. Big-eyed first-graders clung to their mothers, holding fast to the last precious moments of their baby-hood. Two redheaded brothers wearing brand-new yellow shirts that smacked plainly of the first day of school stood uncertainly with their father by the door. The lanky seventh-grader, an old hand at this school business, stood carefully close to the men. The solitary little girl—forti-fied with starch and ringlets—was flushed beet red with excitement and fear. It was 9:05 A.M.

At last, with backward looks and grinding gears, the advance guard of parents withdrew. Without benefit of champagne, the little ship was afloat. Captain and crew faced each other apprehensively.

I placed my hand authoritatively on the school register that lay open on my desk and creakily called the roll. Four families were listed on its first page—three of them with two children each, the fourth with one. Next to the register lay the schedule I had so agonizingly prepared. Seven small faces turned sunflower fashion toward mine. It began to look as if there was nothing to do but start school.

"Well, here we all are," I announced needlessly. "I've seen you around before this, but now it's time for us all to get to know each other. Put your hand up like this when I call your name."

From youngest to oldest, they all raised their hands obediently—the first-graders in awed knowledge that they were in school and still breathing; the older children with a more matter-of-fact curiosity. I then walked to the board and printed MISS MARGOT in large letters.

"That's my name," I explained. "If I were an older teacher, I'd make you call me Miss Pringle because that's my last name. But I'm just like you first-graders. . . ." I waved my hand toward them and they all blinked solemnly. ". . . Because I'm brand new at this school. So you call me Miss Margot and I'll learn your names as fast as I can."

My top drawer produced a crackling cellophane package of balloons. Eyes widened in astonishment.

"Let's see who can blow one of these up first," I suggested, handing them out. It emerged that several children had never seen balloons, but Gene, the seventh-grader, demonstrated the capabilities of his own quite well—and soon the room was full of purple, puffing faces. In a moment six balloons had swelled forth to their fullest dimensions. The seventh belonged to a small first-grader who was on the verge of tears.

"What's the matter, Dick?" I asked.

Dick's straining cheeks deflated and his eyes brimmed over with tears of rage. "I get it just about blowed up every time," he burst out, "and then I just about wet my pants!"

Everybody laughed. Hastily I enlisted someone else to blow up Dick's balloon for him, after which we stowed them all on the porch until recess and turned to work. The ice, at least, was broken.

I handed Gene his seventh-grade reader, which he examined warily. "You can choose whatever story you would like to read today," I told him. He spent the next ten minutes leafing unhappily from page to page, trying to decide which would be the least painful to tackle. At last he settled on a tale of lost hunters in the Canadian bush country. I busied myself with another group of children, but occasional glances at Gene's face told the whole story. He might as well have been lost in the Canadian bush himself.

Later on that morning, he got six out of twenty sixth-grade spelling words right. The picture of Gene as a scholar was beginning to take definite shape.

Pansy and Billy were called on next, to read to me aloud while two of the first-graders cut out animal pictures, and the other two lost themselves in ecstasy over the thrill of abstract art. Our painting "easels" were crude slabs of beaverboard on which we pinned the broad smooth sheets of paper. Our paints were few—tiny jars of orange, green, yellow, and blue, the only colors that had been available in town. No red! Nevertheless, the children's reaction to them was a beautiful sight to behold, as they slapped and splashed the colors in absorbed fascination. I could hardly tear myself away from watching them, but I had to get on with Pansy and Billy, who had opened the easy reader I had given them to the proper page and sat waiting together obediently.

"All right, here we go!" I said, hastily joining them. "Pansy, why don't you read the first page to get us started?"

Pansy's brown curls fell around her face as she bent over the book and began reading swiftly, effortlessly, eloquently.

"Gracious," I thought. "This little girl is just a second-grader and she's marvelous." With reluctance I stopped her at the end of the page to give Billy a turn. His big gray eyes hardened as he clenched the covers of the book.

"The . . . little . . . red . . . hen, uhh—said, 'Then . . . I . . . will take . . . it to the—uhh—mill—my, uh—my . . . myself," he faltered—and painfully traveled across the next few lines, like a barefooted person maneuvering a very rocky road. Letting him stop at the first not-too-obvious chance, I handed the book again to Pansy. She skimmed off like a swallow winging through familiar sky.

"I think maybe that's enough for now," I told them. "You mustn't get all worn out the first day." Pansy's face brightened for a moment with a shy smile, but Billy's remained cold and aloof. One thing was certain— as a third-grader, he was nowhere nearly caught up with this second-grade prodigy, and he mustn't be put where she would discourage him. It is hell for men at any age to be outdone by women. And from the looks of things, this young man would be a tough enough nut to crack without a younger girl outdoing him at every step.

Pansy and Billy went to work making printed signs for objects around the classroom, while I turned to the first grade. The second shift of beginners had begun painting, while the gaudy creations of the first dried on top of the stove—as yet unlit. Both the artists and the paper-cutters were called from their work and gathered around me in one corner, where we had pushed two or three old desks to create a special seating area.

Perched beside me on the rickety seats, the first-graders were an engaging group of four shiny little boys. The two Wells brothers—Dick, who had had the balloon trouble, and Gary, an angelically blond five-year-old—had huge, serious, gray-blue eyes and a look of perpetual wonder. Eddie Jones had red hair and freckles, and a grin that belonged in a hot dog advertisement. My friend Leslie had lost his out-of-school confidence, and wore a wistful expression on his fair, fine-featured face. Four first-graders on their first school day—and men every one of them, from their heads to their snugly blue-jeaned bottoms and heavy-booted toes.

"Today we're going to talk about something I bet you boys know all about," I explained, smiling at their awe of schools and teachers, which was destined to last so short a time. "I wonder if any of you ever saw any wild animals around here—rabbits or deer, or anything. Let's see who can tell about an animal he saw in the last few days before school started."

There was a tongue-tied silence, as four little boys groped for ideas and words. I chattered on. "You know, I've seen lots, and I've only been here a few days. Jackrabbits, and cottontails, too, and the biggest snake that crawled across the road when I drove up here last night. Ooosh, he was a big one! I put on the brakes so I wouldn't run over him and get the tires all ooky."

Interest beamed forth on four faces.

"Prob'ly a bull snake," said Eddie wisely. "They're the biggest."

"The heck they are!" contradicted Leslie. "They got some mighty big ole rattlesnakes right around here. I just about ran over one in my bare feet."

"Yeah," chimed in Pansy from another corner of the room—and I realized that all the other children were listening with fascination. (In a one-room school, everyone is exposed to everyone else's work, and, as a result, sometimes the mouths of babes can put out precocious wisdom.) "Old Leslie, he went over to Gladys's house in his bare feet, and just about stepped right on a rattlesnake in the middle of the road. Papa killed it with a fence post."

Leslie puffed up with the prestige of one who has made a narrow escape.

"Heck," said Dick. "That's nothing. We got lots of snakes at our place, and skunks, too. One night Daddy went out to the bathroom and he stepped right on a skunk."

"Gee," breathed Eddie, his face breaking into wreaths of delight. "I sure wouldn't like to be dashing out the door and step on a *skunk*! I'd stomp on his head!"

Gary allowed as how *he* would have taken a shovel and a pitchfork after that skunk.

"Well," said Dick, warming to his subject, "Daddy went and grabbed his gun, and the skunk ran into the chicken house, and Daddy ran right in the chicken house after him, and shot his head off BANG! BANG! and it stunk like the devil in there a couple of days. The hens wouldn't even go in and lay their eggs." His eyes were wide with pungent memory.

I laughed till the tears ran down my face, and the children stared in astonishment. Dick wore the comical expression of a child who has made a hit and isn't sure just why. He decided to try again.

"One time Daddy chased a bobcat all around our barn," he informed us. "In his stocking feet, too! Pretty soon they was both a-running 'round the barn and pretty soon that bobcat was chasin' Daddy. He chased Daddy all around the Austin barn. Pretty soon Daddy jumped up on top of the barn and up came the bobcat. Oh, he had lots of troubles up at the Austin place."

The mental picture I was forming of Dick's father was a lively one. Later, I learned that there really had been a bobcat at the old Austin place one night, and that Mr. Wells really had gone after it with a rifle without stopping for his boots. But the episode lost nothing in the telling.

Gary, Dick's little brother, had listened with the critical interest of one who knows the truth. Gary had an air of conscious superiority, despite his tender five years, which was to become a real problem.

"Once we all saw a junk when we was comin' out from town," he announced, with a lisp so heavy he was hard to understand. "Daddy must of bumped him 'cause he was 'tinking. He must have come close 'cause he was smelling real plain!"

While Gary was speaking, Dick had been hopping up and down with impatience, and nobody else seemed ready to talk, so I called on him again. He struck a pose and launched into his third tale—this one about mice.

"Mama caught about ten mice in the stove," he told us gleefully. "She shut the door and turned the gas on and when she opened it up *they was gassed to death.*" He paused to let this sink in, then he lowered his voice dramatically. "When Mama went out to the bathroom," he confided importantly, "Gary SNUCK THIS MOUSE TAIL IN THE FRYING PAN! It was some other meat Mama had cooking in there, chicken I guess. Mama came back and when she found out SHE MADE GARY EAT THAT MOUSE TAIL!"

Gary looked at his toes as modestly as if it had all really happened, and I stifled another fit of mirth. The others ooh'd and aah'd, enormously impressed.

Eddie beamed with pleasure. "If he eats a mouse tail," he shouted jubilantly, "then he's a mouse!"

"Yeah," said Leslie knowledgeably. "Maybe he'll get a tail, too. Dogs eat mice. That's how come *they* got tails."

All of a sudden Billy chimed in from his new desk. "You know Doc, that works here on the ranch?" he asked. Everyone nodded. "Daddy says one time old Doc got awful drunk down in Ekalaka. He got so drunk he picked up an old skunk right by the tail and he carried it right in the door of the café down there. He couldn't get to stinkin' till Doc set him down, and Doc said he'd set him down if they wouldn't let him have a free dinner. Them people knew he would do it too, so they sure let him get a dinner, steak and everything. He chucked the skunk out in the bushes."

"And never paid nothing!" finished Eddie.

That was one form of blackmail I had never heard of. I let the first-graders return to their seats. They had been creative enough for one day.

Recess arrived quickly. When it came, we all trooped out to the toilets in a body while I explained that now was the hour to employ them. The girls' toilet, used solely by Pansy and me, was in relatively good condition—it even had a painted lid that shut down neatly, causing the ranch cook to refer to it scornfully as "one of them WPA jobs." The boys' toilet, however, was awful. Its stall not only had plentiful holes in the walls, which promoted a lot of peekaboo foolishness, but was in otherwise bad repair. The seat was full of splinters, and it was also a touch too high for our younger clientele, leading to a definite problem when four or five little boys crowded in together. That was quickly stopped by our first official School Rule—only one boy in the toilet at a time. I asked Gene to supervise that end of things, feeling that he was better suited for it than I. But the boys' toilet remained an unscenic spot, and I was never quite sure what to do about it. During a cold snap in the winter, its removable lid froze solidly shut, making it necessary to send a committee forth with the two school hammers to knock it loose. The lid was propped against the wall from then on, to be superimposed on the framework only in times of actual sit-down need. The yawning pit left by this operation incurred its own hazards, and I left at the end of the year feeling relieved that nobody had fallen in.

Our social studies period followed directly after recess. According to the manual, the beginners at this time were supposed to become better acquainted with the mysteries of school, so we all went outside again for a critical tour of the school grounds—to inventory our meager assets.

"Gene," I told the seventh-grader, "please write down all the things we see out here, so that afterwards we can make a map." Gene's expression showed that he thought this pretty foolish, but he was glad enough to get outside, away from the staring pages of a book. The younger children—thanks to recess and the skunk discussion—had lost most of their self-consciousness and were getting used to the reality that this was school and they were in it. Together we all set forth, through tall dry grass and beggar-lice burrs that infested our socks.

As we circled the grounds, Gene dutifully recorded on his list the outlying buildings and three junk piles that adorned the eastern end of the lot. There was a fence on that side, beyond which gurgled the main irrigation ditch through a thicket of wild roses. We swung around past a dead cottonwood tree, while Gene showed us where the men meant to finish the fence around the schoolyard. The wandering in and out of cattle had disturbed last year's teacher. A dilapidated shed lay beyond the windmill, brimful of broken desks and moldy, mouse-infested books.

Nothing more was found, so we returned inside and I sketched up a rough diagram of what we had seen.

"That's what we have in our schoolyard," I summed up, chalk in hand. "Can anybody think of some things we could do, to fix it a little better?"

The first-graders looked blankly at my chalk-scrawled map, seeing no connection between it and the schoolyard they had just walked around. The other children thought for a moment.

"Papa's going to come up here with a bunch of men on Sunday and work on the school," offered Leslie at last.

"They're going to build the fence and fix up some swings," continued his sister. "Mama says anything you want done up here, that's your chance."

I ignored the implication that I would have only one chance, saying firmly that the men might be coming but that we should think of things ourselves to help them out. After all, this was our school and not the men's, and we wanted to fix it up nicely. *Didn't we?* The floor was open for suggestions.

Gene finally thought he might borrow a tractor to mow the weeds that sprang up throughout the yard. We decided to clean out the shed to see if any of the old books were still useful, and Leslie offered to bring his wagon to haul them to the schoolhouse. Pansy thought we should find something in which to burn our volumes of trash, and Gene recollected where he could find an old oil drum for this purpose. Eddie and Billy Jones volunteered to bring some leftover dabs of blue and green and yellow paint for our many unpainted objects in the schoolroom. And to increase our supplies, we decided to look for old magazines for cutting out, as soon as we could find some.

"Do you think we can do anything to fix up the washstand?" I asked. The washstand, over in one corner of the room, consisted of a spare desk on which sat the metal water dispenser with a nearby basin and bucket. One towel hung limply from a nail, mocking the sanitary regulations in the Board of Health book. I explained that we needed paper towels and some paper cups, and the children agreed it would be a good idea to order them. Meantime we decided that everyone should bring their own drinking cup from home, to avoid the risk of catching cold. We found a battered piece of oilcloth and nailed it under the water dispenser to catch drips, and even fixed up a place on the porch to hang our tools, which luckily were plentiful, and included hammers, a saw, paintbrush and pliers, and a vast assortment of bolts and nails.

The morning passed busily. Just before lunch we put a list up on the blackboard of things we needed from home, which the older children copied for the beginners and themselves. It read:

Varnish	Magazines
Paint	Paintbrushes
Cartons	Orange crates
Oilcloth	Sandpaper
Drinking cups	Wagons

The lists were taken home to slightly perplexed parents, who sent everything they could find—and wondered out loud. The kids were fixing up the schoolhouse all right, but do you suppose they were learning anything?

Probably not!

Lunchtime followed shortly. Hands were washed in a tin basin, each youngster emptying his water into the slop pail under the washstand. Then all went outside to eat their lunches, while Gene initiated them into the art of trading sandwiches for candy, and oranges for cake. Within a day or two, Billy—who had definite gypsy inclinations—was existing on a noontime diet of candy and cake alone. Our second School Rule promptly evolved from a health lesson that extolled the virtues of a balanced diet. All of us should try to bring sandwiches and milk and fruit each day, I told them—and only after that sweets *if* we wanted them. From now on we would have to be very strict about trading; sandwiches for sandwiches only, or fruit for fruit, or cake for candy. But you couldn't trade one kind of thing for another or there would be an end to all trading right away.

I wasn't going to stop them altogether if we could be reasonable, because trading was too much fun. I remembered my own days in the fourth grade at a country school when the thrill of swapping off a dull jelly sandwich for somebody else's ham and cheese, throwing in five peanuts to boot, made noon a time of real adventure—and required no small skill.

The day progressed. Gene's reading in two subjects took him so long that he never got to his composition at all. During the afternoon I sat beside him at his desk, and we both realized that measuring and computing our room area would take almost a week—not one hour, as I had estimated. The first-graders, it turned out, could not count to ten and did not know what any letters or numbers signified—a perfectly normal situation for children that young, though I did not realize it at the time. Billy's handwriting was even worse than his reading, and his arithmetic not much better, while Pansy shone in all subjects, not just reading. With this rough information I could begin to plan realistically for the children's learning. By the time they bolted out the door for home, I felt as if I, at least, had learned something.

The last child vanished in what looked to me like a cloud of golden dust, and I felt suddenly weak with the relief of having the first plunge into teaching over with. I leaned limply against the wall, as shaken up as if I had gone over Niagara Falls in a barrel. Eventually I came to my senses enough to perceive the mess in the schoolroom and feel vaguely obliged to do something about it. With a mouthful of thumbtacks, I gathered up the day's artwork, ascended a chair, and began pinning it up to form a border around the drab tan wall.

Suddenly I heard strange sounds drawing nearer, sounding more and more like gunshots, until something thumped determinedly on the schoolhouse wall. Getting down off the chair, I spat out the thumbtacks and went to investigate. Whoever they were, they were not supposed to knock down my schoolhouse with me in it.

For a moment I saw no one. Then a bewhiskered young man appeared around one corner, followed by a diminutive female who was firing a pistol into the air.

Blinking, I recognized my college roommate, Nona Sutton, returning with her fiancé, Nate Pond, from a mountain climbing jaunt in Wyoming's Wind River Range, and shortly bound back again for the East.

With loud hosannas, I stumbled into their jeep with them. Slightly delirious, we plunged through the river and whizzed through the sixty dusty miles to town. We had a pleasant steak dinner. And we hatched out plans for the most unusual school demonstration to be witnessed in Montana for some time.

CHAPTER THREE

A Visit from Mountain Climbers

Next morning when the children arrived at school, they found an assortment of cut-out pictures of high mountains that I had managed to find in a pile of ancient, mouse-eaten *National Geographics*.

"Did any of you ever go high up into the mountains?" I asked. No, they had not—in fact, several children did not know what mountains were, having grown up in a strictly mountainless area. I explained that mountains were very big hills—they knew about hills—and that if you climbed up a long way, they were all covered with trees. But you could keep on going up, I continued, until it was too cold and high for trees, and then there was nothing but rocks and ice and snow.

We consulted the Alpine pictures I had found and discussed what we would do if we had to climb any place as high and dangerous as one of those mountains.

"You know there are people who like to climb that way just for fun," I explained, "to see if they can do it. They take ropes with them to keep from falling, and they wear sharp spikes in their shoes so they won't slip on the ice. They go way up to the top where they can see for hundreds of miles, so high they are up above the clouds sometimes!"

Everyone was much interested to hear of people who could climb up higher than clouds. At last I asked them, "How would you like to see some people who have really done that?"

"Aw," said Gene. "Ain't none of them around *here*."

"You'd be surprised," I told him. "All of you sit still a minute and I will come back with a real mountain climber."

I opened the door of the teacherage. Nate, who had spent the night outside in his sleeping bag, was now wonderfully arrayed; entwined with ropes, ice axes, and so on, he looked ready to tackle Mount Everest. The month's growth of whiskers he had acquired in the Wind River wilderness added to the effect as he clanked and jingled into the classroom.

Seven mouths popped open in astonishment. Nate gave a fine lecture on mountain climbing, explaining the uses of this various equipment. His nylon rope fascinated Gene. The little boys touched his spike-bottomed shoes with wonder. He gave Billy, for keeps, an ironclad spike or "piton," used for anchoring ropes after being pounded into place on some sheer rock cliff. Recovering their tongues, the children asked many questions.

At last I asked them, "Now would you like to meet a lady mountain climber?"

Nona entered, to their even greater astonishment. "These people have been climbing mountains in Wyoming," I explained, "and now that they are here, they want to show you how they do it. We haven't any mountains so we'll just have to pretend that the schoolhouse is one. Let's get up and go quietly outside."

We filed outdoors while the experts stayed inside to make a final check of equipment. In a moment they joined us, and Nate tossed a loop of rope up around the chimney. Deftly he clambered around the overhanging eave and pulled himself up until he was standing Superman-fashion upon the roof. Nona followed him up, and those of us earthbound craned our necks in admiration. It looked so easy. They had popped up there in no time!

"Now let's go around to the other side," I told the children, "and watch how they come down."

Coming down employs an art known as rappelling, in which the rope is passed around the body and under the bottom to slide down at breakneck speed. Thump-bump-bump, and Nate stood on the ground beside us. Thump-bump-bump, and Nona joined him. The rope was flipped off the chimney and neatly recoiled. The show was over.

Packing all supplies into their jeep, the mountain climbers departed for the East amid a seven-child ovation.

Our art and language activities centered around this event for several days. The first grade composed a story about it, which read:

> Two strangers came to school.
> They were climbers.
> He put a rope around the chimney

And climbed all the way up.
She tied a rope around her
And up she went too.
Then they came down the schoolhouse
Hippity hoppity down.

I printed a large chart of this story, which we read out loud several times a day, as I moved the pointer under the words, until the beginners knew it by heart. Through this exercise, four children gained their first understanding that printed words say something, and before long all could show me the way you go across the lines from left to right, then drop down to the next one. Soon they could pick out a few words by shape alone. For formal reading, which requires this type of groundwork, it was not a bad beginning.

Months later I learned that the community had been scandalized by tales the children took home concerning their second school day. Word quickly spread to the superintendent's office in town. What a dreadful thing to do to the schoolhouse! Fortunately the superintendent only smiled, and in blissful ignorance of any sensation, we at the schoolhouse went on with our business.

The matter of reading, and how it should be taught, soon loomed as a major issue. The parents did not realize or understand the value of preliminary work such as what we were doing with the mountain climber story. They felt impatiently that their boys should begin reading from a book at once and said a great deal on the subject at home, little realizing how faithfully four small reporters kept me informed on their sentiments. With artless regularity the boys repeated what they had heard at home, and their reports troubled me. "Papa says we should of gone to that other school. Papa says it's too bad they ain't got a teacher that knows what she's doing around here. Papa says Aunt Betty's kids on Star Creek is starting to read already. Papa says if we can't write our names before Thanksgiving he is going to take us out of here."

I knew from my training at Cornell that the little boys were not ready to read yet, no matter what the teacher on Star Creek was doing. Results of reading readiness tests I gave the first week showed that none of the first-graders were ready. Gary, the five-year-old, scored as a poor risk for first-grade work; in many ways he would have benefited from waiting to start school until the following year. Leslie and Dick, the next highest, landed in the Low Normal category, seriously lacking the background understanding of words and sentences, and the ability to notice details, that are both so necessary for reading success. Eddie ranked highest, barely squeaking into the "normal" category for which six weeks of readiness training is still recommended.

In fact the only sign on the tests of unusual capability had been the results of the "Draw a Man" section. The more anatomically complete the drawing was, the higher was the rating of the child. Tests came back minus legs and arms, or faces and fingers—but all had remarkably accurate reproductive organs. There was nothing in the manual to help interpret that skill.

I tried to explain the situation regarding reading readiness to parents, but nothing seemed to do much good. The county superintendent backed my program, so I just went ahead with it, while disparaging comments from parents kept trickling in. It seemed that the only solution for eliminating comparison to "Aunt Betty's kids" would be to shoot them, or their teacher—for whom I was developing a healthy dislike.

In late October I met a first-grade teacher in town, who reassured me. *Her* children couldn't write their names or say the alphabet either. I became righteously indignant.

As for the promised repairs to the schoolhouse, the men did come on the Sunday that Leslie and Pansy had prophesied. In fact, the entire community came, and I was surprised to see that our lonesome hills concealed so much humanity. The schoolchildren came too, with all eight parents and six younger brothers and sisters. Seven employees from the main SH Ranch also showed up, including general ranch hands, the cowboy Forrest Liberty, and two men who worked for the outfit part-time and raised wheat on shares during the other part. Doc, of skunk-related fame in the children's stories, was there. And a few neighboring families filled out the group to form a sizable gathering.

The men finished building the fence and dragged the old shed inside the yard, so my saddle horse would have a place for shelter when the blizzards came. The foundations of the schoolhouse were patched up, and a few heavy poles constructed into a frame for swings and a teeter-totter, while children screamed and fought and threw things at each other, and Billy took it upon himself to kick dirt into all the newly dug postholes. Inside, the women piled up a sumptuous array of chicken, sandwiches, salad, and baked beans. I began to see why community work days were so popular.

By three o'clock most of the work was finished, and the gathering broke into small talkative groups. A large car pulled up to the gate, out of which climbed the main ranch owner, Ed Love, and several women. I was interested in meeting them as they toured around the school-yard to survey our progress, for the owner had much influence in our community.

Mr. Love, a Ford dealer, lived in town and visited his new ranch house on weekends only. The ranch was different from others along the river, because it raised a good deal of wheat in addition to cattle. The work was done by several tenant families whose dwellings dotted the ranch and whose children attended the school. Mr. Love lent money and machinery to his farmers, some of whom had been on the place for years. Owner and tenants split their yields of hay and grain. I had wondered why the school was so deeply located in the midst of a private ranch, bearing its name, and so far from a county road. I now learned that Mr. Love had bought the schoolhouse and moved it out there two years previously, to enable tenant families with growing children to stay on site. Many of the families, indebted to him, found it profitable to remain in any case. The situation was slightly reminiscent of feudalism. Once I grasped how the place operated, I had clearer understanding of Mr. Love's local importance, including the widespread knowledge of every move he made.

I had a pleasant chat with Mr. Love and the ladies, who were curious about my desertion of the distant East in favor of so unscenic a part of the West as this one. I explained that I had always wanted to teach a country school and that my fondness for horses and cattle made Montana a likely place to begin.

"Well, there's nothing like a pretty schoolmarm to pep things up," commented Mr. Love as they departed. "Look out for that new cowboy I just hired, though. He's a pretty smooth guy." I would only later discover the charms of that new cowboy, who was to become my husband.

The electricity went off a few nights after the schoolhouse work bee, leaving me unable to cook or do much else by the light of my solitary candle. I resolved to go down to the main ranch and invite myself to supper, thereby learning some more about the place and its operation. The main ranch, in addition to Mr. Love's house, had corrals, a cookhouse, and a bunkhouse where the hired hands lived. It also had one end of the go-devil or cable car that went across the river to the main road to town. And it had a cast of characters all its own, ranging from Doc to Fuzzy, who also rode a motorcycle, to a slightly alcoholic cow boss and a cook whose reputation for tongue lashings was widely known. I was welcomed in to supper, however, with grand hospitality. We dined by candlelight, and I began to feel as if I were watching a Broadway comedy. My father, in far-away Washington, D.C., thought I should write a one-act play to immortalize these characters, but this did not happen.

CHAPTER FOUR

A Pumpkin Party

Getting to know my seven kids became the most absorbing game in the world as we settled into as regular a classroom routine as I could muster. I experienced a never-ending delight in listening to them talk among themselves and in watching their wide-eyed thrill at any new discovery. The first-grade boys were particularly endearing. As we read stories and talked about local happenings, learned rhymes, and played games, it seemed a ceaseless challenge to understand them better and find ways of teaching them more. At an easy pace, they went through most of the readiness work for reading. Before long they would tackle books themselves, and I knew the process would be so much easier if they liked school and were having fun.

It seemed my plan was starting to take hold. When muddy roads kept the Wells boys home one day, they cried and put up a great fuss at not going to school. Dick even fetched his lunch pail and volunteered to trudge the four miles back and forth in his big overshoes. (Usually he and Gary only walked home.) But then talk began to go around that they were having too much fun, the local feeling being that school was like medicine—the worse it tasted the more good it did.

The muddy weather, in fact, led to an interesting day. After pouring in sheets for twenty-four hours, the rain rendered the road a sticky swamp. You could sink to your ankles in gumbo on the hills themselves. By 9:00 in the morning the rain had stopped and the wind was shrieking around the eaves of the schoolhouse. I waited expectantly—no kids! It was a very strange feeling. The cold wind and swirling gray sky made it very plain that winter was a-comin' in.

At about 10:30 Gene finally hove into view, his big feet sucking laboriously in and out of the boggy road. The two of us forgot about school, spending the morning chinking cracks on the sagging porch and nailing board shutters over the leaky porch windows. Next day all the children were back at school, and Leslie had a breathless tale to tell of getting stuck with his wagon near the Hirsch house. "We was figgerin' to go up the road," he reported, "and then we figured not to! The wagon just sunk. I was a-pushin' and a-pullin', went and got the shovel. Zzzzz, and the wheels caught on and pretty soon they started to roll. Zzzz! We had to jack the wagon up, finally got her out, though. Wowie!" He shook his head disgustedly.

Leslie had blossomed in school the past week or two—since developing a warm friendship with Eddie. His parents were relieved. Before that, he had told them school wasn't much fun anymore and it went on too long; he didn't think he wanted to go.

Dick had had trouble with the mud, too. "We started chuggin' out the gate," he told us, "and when I got out to shut it my feet went clear down so far I couldn't get 'em out! Grandpa thought he'd have to pull me out with the chain!" His eyes widened. "But I tugged and tugged, and finally up they came and my overshoes was down in the hole."

Dick's troubles with the other children at recess were spotlighted when a little survey showed that none of them wanted to play with him. He was too bad a loser—too quick to quit and feel hurt. In schoolwork he could never be pushed. He wanted desperately to be the best and to win praise, and the slightest reprimand sent him into tears. If he wasn't reassured all the time he got flustered and tense, forgetting everything.

Now that the children had turned against him, I decided to talk to his mother. "He's got to be the center of attention," she told me. "I don't know why, but you can't scold him, he just dies. You've got to just love him along, I guess."

He was a marvelously bright and sensitive little boy. The best system seemed to be encouragement and reassurance. And it worked, for as Dick grew more secure, his troubles with the other children dissolved.

Dick also continued to be the most expressive of the lot, forever coining phrases of his own. Once, when using a small plastic tool to extract thumbtacks, he commented, "This damn pitchfork ain't so hot."

Another time, pondering social truths, he mused aloud, "Now a bachelor lives in an old shack all by himself and he didn't get married either." He paused. "A man, he works all day and a woman takes care of the kids. Then when the man comes home, the woman goes to work. I don't see where that woman gets any rest."

His southern accent and slight lisp made everything he said slightly funnier, along with his wide-eyed earnestness. Another time he was hanging around indoors at recess, so I suggested he try to catch some of the water bugs in the tank outside for our aquarium. He returned in a few minutes with two of them in a glass jar, announcing indignantly, "If you want any more bugs you can go get 'em yo'self." One had bitten his finger.

Eddie, with his engaging grin, soon drew to the lead in first-grade work, enchanted when he finally succeeded in writing his name. "Now we's getting down to WORK!" was his joyful comment. Interested in mechanical things, he found delight in watching the second hand of my clock, and he viewed the workings of a fountain pen as a real puzzle. "I like this color pen," he decided. "It's not black anyway—I don't like black. You can put ink in it! It's got an ink place. I think it's got a little button in there like what can hold ink. I think when you put the ink in, the button goes across real fast and keeps the ink in."

A moment later, opening his lunch pail, he was chanting, "Eat my sandwich, jump jump jump! Drink my milk, jump jump jump! Put on my overshoes, jump jump jump! Run out there and beat old Dick!"

Eddie, for a six-year-old, was a real man of the world, and he swore like a trooper. One day a deafening crash rang out through the relatively quiet schoolroom. Everyone jumped. Eddie had been returning a library book when he bumped into the dictionary table, upsetting the entire pile of teetering volumes on top of himself.

"Christ Jesus!" he exploded, crawling out of the wreckage.

I looked at him in as forbidding a fashion as possible, saying, "Eddie, around here we just don't say things like that." He shot me a quizzical glance and returned to his seat. That afternoon, when he was painting a picture, he wore such an enormous ear-to-ear grin, I became suspicious.

"Eddie," I queried, "what's so funny?"

"Aw, nothin'," he said with a shrug. The grin became wider as he studied his paintbrush. "Oh, it's just a lady in that book," he finally confessed.

All eyes were now on him. With the air of one telling a marvelous joke he cried, "SHE AIN'T NO GOOD!"

"Why not, Eddie?"

"Oh, she just ain't got nothing on at all, only here and here!"

He continued to giggle and grin the rest of the afternoon. At recess I consulted the magazine he had indicated. There was a full-page colored photograph of some candidate for "The American Venus," clad in four carefully placed grapes and a banana.

Eddie stood out on other occasions, too, such as the time when the children all called him a "Wobble Chin." We had read a poem together with a "Wobble Chin Lady" in it, and Eddie did not appreciate being called by that name. But he was usually easy to pacify, as when he came wailing into the classroom one noon.

"What happened, Eddie?"

"Billy stepped on my head."

"How did he step on your head?"

"With his overshoe."

"What was your head doing so Billy could step on it?"

"Well, Leslie tripped me, so I went to get up and Billy stepped on me."

"Did he do it on purpose?"

"Yes. He just stepped on it."

"Oh dear. Is there a big bump there?"

"No, but it hurts. The radio says you can't fight, only with kids your own age." Eddie's source of information had been a Miles City radio program for children. He hung up his coat and went to play with blocks. In a minute he piped up, "Hey, Miss Margot—see my big toughie?" He proudly showed me the bump that was now visible on his head.

Inexperienced with children as I was, I got a kick out of such goings-on—and had fun, too, concocting various devices to help them learn. Instructional methodology books were full of these tricks of the trade—everything from reading games to number charts and a homemade abacus made with wooden beads strung on a wire coat hanger. The challenge of keeping some children busy at their seats while I was working with others was ever present, especially with the little ones who tired easily and could not yet read. Sets of little cards with bird and animal pictures to match up, homemade puzzles, and envelopes with pictures of similar-sounding objects to sort and classify—there were so many things to construct, and the midnight hour more than once found me still cutting pictures out of magazines and pasting them on small squares of paper. My fingers also wore, before long, the purple trademark of a teacher: hectograph ink from the sticky gelatin duplicator, which reluctantly turned out copies of extra lessons—and a glorious mess.

Before too long, the supplies we ordered from the catalog began to come in, and opening the heavy cartons was as big a thrill as Christmas. We got our paper cups and a mirror to hang by the washstand so the children could see their faces. A fancy felt-pointed lettering pen made it a joy to print out the large charts needed for teaching early reading. Beautiful new readers and workbooks arrived for each child, along with paste, scissors, and colored paper. There was clay, and penmanship paper, and, best of all, eight big jars of paint. The bright colors sent Gary—whose daily plea had been "Teacher, I wish I could paint!"—into ecstasies. Our border of artwork above the blackboard blossomed into newer, richer, and wilder designs. And the paint-smeared urchins, after one trip home, were protected henceforth in "smocks"—made from old workshirts worn backwards (and my college house-party beer jacket).

Our need for library books was acute. I leapt with pleasure at the chance to borrow books from the State Extension Library, which performed so wonderful a service to rural schools. All you did was send to the library a description of the students' ages and grades, mentioning also any special interests or other requests of your own. In a week or two, there arrived in the mail a large selection of books hand-picked by one of the state librarians. You could keep them for several months or return them for another selection as soon as you liked. The only charge was the return postage.

We delayed opening our books until we had fixed up a place to put them. Our one bookcase was in sorry shape, hammered together by last year's teacher out of splintery planks. We hauled it outdoors and propped it against the schoolhouse for consideration. Paint, we decided, it had to have. But paint was scarce, and its rough, dirty surface would absorb a great deal more than a smooth one. We decided on a good scrubbing, followed by sandpapering and a going-over with a borrowed carpenter's plane.

The job proceeded in shifts for a day or two. Two children at a time went out to work with the plane or sandpaper while others recited with me inside. If they cut up or fooled around out there, they forfeited their chance to work. Quickly the beginners developed an adult and workmanlike attitude, tiptoeing inside to change places or keeping me posted on the progress outside.

Billy was not used to so much freedom. From two years' school experience, he had developed the attitude that you get away with anything you can. Whenever asked to do something, his face clouded with hatred of school, hatred of authority. In a large class he could have caused a lot of trouble, but here one was too easily caught. Sullen and resistant, he stared into space when spoken to—and recited with the manner of one who, at gunpoint, has no other choice. Rumors about Billy and his brother had warned that they were wild and uncontrollable "little hellions." With Eddie I had no trouble, but Billy was a hostile and unhappy little boy.

On the second day we worked on the bookcase, Billy disrupted the classroom twice by bolting to the window and crying, "LOOK! Here comes Timber and Wallace!" when the two cowboys passed on horseback. Scolded, he was sullenly copying spelling words at his seat when recess came and we all went to admire the progress of the bookcase. Smoothed and planed as well as possible, it was ready to be painted, and I went inside with Dick to stir up our meager paint supply. When we returned, great beaverlike gouges had appeared in the top plank and telltale shavings oozed from the plane. Billy was playing with the others. I called him.

"Do you know anything about this?" I asked. His eyes hardened, and he said nothing.

Meanwhile, the other children were fuming. "I just *hate* that Billy for doing that!" burst out Dick, close to tears. The others came and repaired the damage as best they could, while Billy poked his lip out in I-Don't-Care silence. In a private talking-to, moments later, he burst into bitter sobbing. "I just hate school!" he cried. "I just HATE IT!"

I found myself thinking about Billy a lot, wondering what had made him so angry and what could be done about it. Punishing him was useless. He had been punished so much it rolled right off him. It was also useless to kill him with kindness. Nothing worked.

Gene, such a star and hero on the playground, was strangely dimmed when faced with an open book. His suffering resistance was quiet and passive, never assertive, showing itself only as a dead expression on his face and an apparent lowering of metabolism rate to the hibernation level. In an attempt to change this, I searched high and low for topics that might interest him—and launch him on a slow upward spiral in school. He was interested in machines, he revealed in a brief composition. He wanted to quit school and go to work in the wheat fields.

That was a lead. In our social studies book, a chapter dealing with geography gave information about the American wheat belt. We skipped to it and started there. He was sent home with questionnaires about the wheat raised on our own ranch—what kind was it; how much was grown; how was it planted and fertilized and harvested? We sent away for free materials from national baking industries, and studied the uses of different wheats—the milling processes they underwent, ways they were transported, flours and feeds they produced. In arithmetic, yields per acre and prices and cash returns were computed from wheat sales on the SH, and Gene made a graph showing the number of box cars that would be filled with one year's production of our grain. After receiving an informative letter from our Custer County agricultural agent, who had promptly answered the one Gene had written to him during a language period, we discussed ways of raising wheat on dry and irrigated land, and whether such processes were good or bad for the soil.

There were different kinds of wheat, just as there were different kinds of cattle, I explained to Gene, after discovering that his family and neighbors had not heard of the wheat varieties developed for conditions in our area of Montana. We examined state bulletins that described these variations and explained where they should be used. Such wheats were selected and bred for high production, I told him, getting into the troublesome area of how plants—or animals for that matter—are bred. He had seen animals mating many times but could not picture plants undergoing the same process! We branched off into the complex field of genetics and reproduction—how cells join up with cells—and I wondered if I was not getting into rather deep water with Gene, who had never heard of cells. We held onion skins against the window, squinting our eyes in the hopes of seeing individual cells, as I explained to him that what we really needed was some kind of magnifying device.

I had an idea, based on much reading about community schools, that if you sent the children home with new ideas, the parents would be interested. I pictured the county agent at our school some evening, addressing a gathering of parents about the newest finds in wheat raising—all an outgrowth of my work with Gene in the classroom. I envisioned, over a period of years, the prosperity of these people increasing, because of engagement with new ideas that had come to them indirectly through their children's school. I saw our little school as a possible starting point for everything good that people search and strive for—a better way of life, through community study and fun gatherings and concerted effort toward building structures such as bridges across the river, which all wanted but none could do alone. I knew such things could be done because they had been done many times in many places poorer and more remote than this one. With the right kind of leadership, a scattered rural community could merge into a conscious, working team.

I made the mistake a lot of young enthusiasts make, thinking this could be done quickly—and by a newcomer. But it wasn't so easy. One day Gene would be interested in school, and then the next day return with a reserved suspicion. After all, what could a schoolmarm know about wheat? I was a teacher, and a dude, and a woman—three fatal strikes. The farmers would take care of the farming. Never mind that I had graduated from Cornell—a famous four-year college of agriculture!

Nevertheless, Gene's increased interest made the project worthwhile, and the materials we collected proved at least that there were other things in print than deadly text books and the local newspaper.

In an effort to appeal to the interests of my young students, I made much of the science corner. Bill and Eddie brought hop toads on the second day of school, and we made them as comfortable as possible in a big coffee can with a rock to sit on and lots of moss in the shallow water. The goldfish were acclimatized by now in a large glass tank full of sand and plants—and Dick's water bugs. Their traveling jar had been taken over by ants dug from our school yard, who made prodigious tunnelings along the glass where we could watch, and used bits of colored paper we suppled for all kinds of underground engineering.

Our next additions were a mouse and a spotted salamander contributed by the ranch hands. The salamander was a fearsome creature, with a reptilian tail and yellow eyes that stuck out of his head on pegs. I assured the children he wasn't poisonous, but we knew little else about him since we lacked the reference books for identification. We experimented with diets and habitats. Billy was adding sand one day and almost buried him, when I hurried to the rescue.

"Take it easy, Bill," I directed. "We don't want any unhappy lizards!"

Our first field trip took place with all the fanfare of a polar expedition—or so it seemed. We set forth ready for anything, taking cans, jars, paper bags, and an enormous shovel that Eddie insisted on dragging behind him. The Wells boys had prepared themselves even further. They arrived at school with large coffee cans nailed to the ends of long pieces of lath, shouldering the gadgets like flags. Three bruised fingers attested to the work that had gone into making them.

"What have you there, boys?" I asked.

Dick's tone of reply scorned my ignorance: "Butterfly nets."

We cut across the fields and down to the river, following a long route home to the school. It wasn't a particularly stellar expedition, as we netted nothing more exciting than more bugs and a variety of uprooted plants, most of which died. It did ignite a new passion, though, that of smashing rocks to see the textures and colors inside, and subsequent recesses were filled with the pounding of hammers by young geologists, who gripped their tools with both hands and applied them with eyes screwed shut in expectation.

After the science hike I encouraged the children to talk about what they had seen. Most of them were too tired to say much. Eddie had been impressed by the "tin can lights" he saw on the way home— reflected from the can he was carrying. Dick chortled, "That jackrabbit—all of us kids took after him. If we'd have caught him, we'd really have fun wouldn't we? Might find him in somebody's desk or somebody's clothes closet."

The science menagerie got along fine until the escape of the mouse, at which point the following story evolved, child-inspired and largely child-composed:

Once upon a time, in the shed at the S H School, there lived a mouse. He was a little mouse, with big brown eyes and a long tail. He lived peacefully with his brother and sister mice among the books and papers in the old shed. And if boys and girls tiptoed in very quietly, they used to hear the mice squeak-squeaking behind the wallboards.

Then one terrible day there was a big noise out in the old shed. The children from the SH School had started to clean the shed. Bang bang, holler holler—such a noise. The mice looked at each other and wiggled their long whiskers. The big mice said to each other, "We better get the heck out of here!" But one little mouse was so scared he couldn't make a move.

Crash bang! went the books in the old shed. Squeak squeak! went Leslie's wagon hauling books to the fire. And all of a sudden one little mouse went straight up in the air—Gene had grabbed his tail.

Into the schoolroom the mouse went. Under a glass jar and a book. Into a coffee can. And some time during the still, dark night *one little mouse got away.*

Into the teacher's soup cans he went. Scritch, scratch into the teacher's wall board. Clitter clatter along the teacher's shelf. Rattle rattle in the teacher's groceries. Dig dig he made a hole, and soon the little mouse was quite at home.

Then, one sad morning, the teacher saw something in the slop pail. Two little ears stuck up out of the water. One little tail floated on top. He had fallen in the water and he had been drowned.

The story was nothing if not true. I poured the dead mouse over the fence with real regret, and the children, fascinated by his sad and mournful ending, made me read their story aloud until we knew it by heart.

The old shed was newly tenanted before long by my gray mare, Orphan Annie, whom Timber (aka Forrest Liberty) and I fetched in the ranch pickup from her summer pasture upriver at Birney one Sunday.

Ever since I had bought her from a cannery sale two years earlier, she had repaid me with grateful service. Her arrival was hailed by the children as a happy increase in our enrollment, and indeed she spent much time during school hours peering into the schoolroom window. We became quite used to the sight, just outside, of two pointed gray ears above an alert, bright-eyed face. During recess she did her best to join in games the children played, and it took repeated chasings-away to make her stay at her own end of the lot.

When Annie arrived she was lame in one front leg, and Doc was right on hand with a remedy. "Just sew her leg up inside a piece of old inner tube," he instructed, "not too awful tight but just enough so it'll draw. It'll fix her up in no time, why that leg'll come out just like the other one."

It never did to laugh at Doc. I asked him respectfully if a tire-patching kit would do the job as I wasn't too good at sewing rubber. Luckily both front legs eventually came out alike without the use of such drastic measures.

Winter was coming, and the wind that whistled through the shed made it a shelter of dubious value. Liberty offered to help me cover the whole building with tar paper. His sole time off was during the evenings after supper, so the two of us spent much time hammering and pounding by flashlight at the end of the schoolyard—and rumors began to fly around the ranch concerning "that cowboy," and his late horseback returns to the main ranch from the school. I worried about these whisperings for a time, and then became annoyed. The job had to be done, and its hours were not a matter of choice.

Once fall had advanced, making it necessary to leave my car across the river, I was able to get around the neighborhood on Annie. An arrangement with Mrs. Hirsch made it possible for me to send her my laundry in a sack and for me to iron some of her things along with my own in return. My once-a-week laundry visits to the Hirsches' brought welcome relief from my own non-cooking and entailed some lively gallops down the dirt road to their house. The journey home was slower, through the full dark. I learned how silently a horse's hoofs can sound along the grass at night, and saw for the first time stars shining up from the depths of mud puddles scattered along the way. The schoolhouse—dark and aloof by starlight—was so forbidding a prospect that I began leaving a bedside lamp on to welcome me home. Still, unsaddling Annie and feeding her in the dark night, then going into my own little empty teacherage, was one of the lonely times.

Once or twice as I approached the schoolhouse, I heard the heralding neigh of another horse, and knew that my cowboy helper was there before me. Never before or since has a whinny sounded so musical nor since then have the staccato flames of a coal stove made me rush to the door, mistaking them for hoofbeats drawing nearer through the night.

Going after Timber's saddlehorse another Sunday at a ranch near Miles City, the two of us, and another cowboy, rode five miles of high, pink-and-golden distance without crossing a fence before we spotted the horses we were after. They fanned out in a rainbow of galloping colors, beautiful on the run with the sun shining off their hides, as we headed them back toward the corrals,. Weeks later I went along on a three-day drive with some ranchers who were taking a herd of young cows to a railroad shipping point. Watching some three hundred of them crowd around a reservoir for water, I reflected that the West might be dying—but it was not dead. A day later those same cattle flattened half a mile of barbed-wire fence, stampeding away from their first experience with a concrete highway. Traffic was held up for half an hour while two frantic riders galloped up and down the edges of the road, trying to gather this scattered and rebellious herd and corral it into the pens across the road.

But I missed all the fun, miles away inside the walls of my schoolroom.

A new project was being born, amidst frosty—and rather puny— pumpkins, and the approaching night of Halloween. A play, written by ourselves, could serve many purposes. Swiftly the plans went ahead.

We designed a short skit that fitted our assortment of ages, sexes, and sizes. Pansy, obviously, had to be the witch. Gene, in his gangling approach to six feet, was a natural for a sheet-clad ghost. Four first-grade boys were ideally suited to be goblins. And Billy, I felt, might gain more from playing the starring role of villain and hero than from anything else that had happened to him so far that year.

The plot was simple, almost simple-minded. A bad boy—Billy—ran away from home one night, making vigorous speeches about hating his parents. It happened to be Halloween. In the woods near his home he was badly frightened by a series of spooks, including a witch, who convinced him he should return home. The play ended dramatically with the revelation that that the bad boy would never be bad again.

Silly as it was, the story appealed to the children. They composed their own parts as far as possible. The first grade took to its goblin role with alacrity. Leslie was the Green Goblin, Eddie the Yellow Goblin, Dick the Blue Goblin, and Gary—tiniest and toughest—the Red Goblin. We composed and printed a large chart with the following chant:

> We are the goblins red and blue
> We're going to kick a hole in you!
> We are the goblins yellow and green
> We're going to make you scream scream scream!

Each goblin composed for himself a line or so to say in dire threat to the unfortunate bad boy. Leslie led off with a fearful sneer, saying, "I'm a green goblin and you better get out of here because I'M TOUGH!" Eddie followed with the immortal lines, "I'm a yellow goblin and I'm going to pull your hair, I don't like you 'cause you're so MEAN!" Dick bounded in with a shrill "I'm a blue goblin and you go home before I EAT YOU UP!" And Gary, in alarmingly realistic fashion, rushed in last with a blurted, "I'M A BIG RED GOBLIN AND I'M GOING TO PINCH YOUR NOSE OFF!"

He pinched Billy's nose good and hard, too, every chance he got. Gary was our smallest and youngest. He was also our comic relief, wagging his blond head and issuing wisecracks far beyond his years. As immature in school as Gary was, he was a sharp little boy and he held his own. Billy had tripped him on the playground one day and sent him tumbling full length on his face, at which point Gary had wasted little time in complaining and tears. A few days later it was a wailing Billy who entered the schoolhouse at recess. Gary had waited his chance, and had methodically whacked him over the head with a heavy stick.

In school one day when my back was turned, Gene had thrown a paper wad across the room. Gary, with unutterable scorn, observed, "Hmph. You a *big* boy." His sarcasm was marvelous.

Preparation for the play included scenery and costumes. The scenery was simply a few large trees painted on regular art paper. The costumes were more artistic, or at any rate, more trouble. We obtained gunny sacks and flour sacks as basic materials, and set to work on them as determinedly as if they had been silks and velvets.

Pansy's witch costume was a cloak of black drapery, topped off by a pointed hat. We sewed four flour sacks together, dyed them black, and left a hole to stick her head through. The hat was made from a ring of cardboard and a piece of black paper rolled into a point.

Gene's costume—a sheet—needed no preparation; nor did Billy's, whose everyday clothes fitted his bad boy role well enough! The goblins, however, needed some garbing. The first step was to dye their respective gunny sacks green, yellow, red, and blue. This process filled a full Friday afternoon, running concurrent with regular arithmetic and science work. The shift system was again used, but we all had to stop work to admire each fresh color as it emerged from its dripping bath. Leslie and Gary, as the red and green goblins, had better luck than the other two—red and green taking better on the coarse burlap. Each goblin also had a square head scarf, dyed along with the gunny sack. And these scarves came out pretty enough to suit everyone.

Tailoring the goblin costumes was the next problem, solved by cutting holes in the bottom of each sack for bare legs to poke out, and belting the affair snugly around the waist. Pins held it in place on top, above holes likewise cut for arms; and the whole was topped off by the bright scarves tied into pixie-like points. When the time came to try these on, the entire group was stricken with embarrassment at the idea of taking off its jeans. We needed a guinea pig badly and none would volunteer. At last Eddie and Dick withdrew together into the teacherage, and behind the closed door we heard volumes of shrieks and coy giggling. They remained inside for a full five minutes—overly long, it seemed to me.

"Anything wrong in there?" I called. There was a panic-stricken silence. Then the door burst open and Dick shot forth, the sack draping down from his waist, white legs twinkling as he catapulted around the schoolroom and disappeared inside the teacherage again, slamming the door.

We all had a good laugh at the whirlwind fashion show.

A party at the school on the Friday night before Halloween was arranged to make necessary preparations and work out the lighting system. I felt that the school should be a place of extracurricular activity whenever possible, but this was much limited by the scattered nature of our community and long distances between the families' homes and the school. I drove a total of twenty-four miles that night: twelve to pick all the children up and another twelve to take them home. The disfavor of particular parents made me nervously aware that they must get back promptly, and our resulting hurried session at the school was all too short. Nevertheless, we invented a beautiful orange fire for the witch scene, and a blue lantern for Gene—made of a "trouble light" supplied by me, and a piece of old blue crepe paper. For the goblin scene we laid the trouble light on the floor, where it would throw big black shadows on the wall reflecting the hopping and yowling goblins. A spotlight was made from my bedside lamp and a long roll of corrugated cardboard.

Rehearsals grew feverish as Halloween approached. The goblins nearly put Billy's eye out in rehearsal. Pansy and Billy sweated at home and at school over their laboriously self-copied parts. Recklessly we decided to have a dance in the schoolroom after the play, and posters and invitations went out to this effect—adorned with Gary's gloriously surrealistic pumpkins and Bill's painful printing announcing what he had dubbed "The Punkin Party."

The goblins, in conversation period, produced the following comments, later written down:

Gosh. Everybody'll see our costumes. I'm gonna stay in there! Hide under the bed, under the pillow! Do like that mouse and get in the slop bucket!

Audience is going to sit in the desks. Billy's got to stand up. Gene puts his hand on Billy's shoulder and Billy's supposed to hit him. We better get the pot fixed up so Pansy can chuck him in the stew. I like that part.

We planned to put a real jack-o'-lantern in each window, which delighted the children. Out of their chants around the schoolroom at different times, I pieced together the following ditty, which they repeated gleefully:

Pum pum pum
Punkin with a tongue
Punk punk punk
Sitting in the window.

Punkin punkin
Looking in the mirror
Punkin punkin
Laughing his head off.

Punkin punkin
Looking at the sea,
Punkin punkin
Looking at me!

Punkin sitting on the ceiling
Eating his punkin pie!
Punkin punkin singing his head off,
Winking his punkin eye!

I was given all the pumpkins I wanted at the main ranch, and the night before the play found me on my ever-faithful gray mare, carrying two pumpkins in a gunny sack up to the Wells boys—who had none of their own.

Gene, as master of ceremonies, prepared a greeting that, after countless changings, recopyings, and respellings, looked like this:

We are glad that you folks could come tonight. We hope you can stay for the dance after the show. The play has been written by the school. Every person in the play made his own part. Each person made his own costumes. Staging was done by the school. We would like to thank the people that furnished the lights, sheets, wire, gunny sacks and pumpkins.

The play stars Bill Jones as Fred Smith, a bad little boy of 8 years. Freddie had just ran away from home. Because it is Halloween night he runs in to six spooks who scare him half to death. The first spooks he runs across are 4 goblins. The fifth spook is the witch who just about boils him up. The sixth spook is the ghost who helps him change his mind.

We hope you enjoy the play.

With some final repairs on grammar and spelling, I marked Gene's paper with fat red lines at the end of each sentence, and we practiced reading it aloud. "The red lines," I told him, "mean stop. You always stop when you get to the end of a sentence; that's why the periods are there. No wonder you got all winded reading out loud, if you never stopped at the end of a sentence."

Over and over it we went, working for slower, more comprehensible diction. I knew Gene would be more amenable to working on something he had written himself. Bit by bit, his delivery improved. The fat red lines had helped.

On the day of the play, I was still at the last minute frantically carving pumpkins. The cast arrived with its families, and I whisked the schoolchildren away into the teacherage, hustling them into costumes and sitting them firmly on my bed, threatening dire damage to the first person who moved or cut up. Our curtains—a pair of sheets strung on a wire across the front of the schoolroom—cleared the floor by about eleven inches, making clearly visible to the audience the feet of any figure who walked behind. One of the bolder baby brothers of a cast member escaped from his parents in the audience and crawled underneath the curtain, across the stage, and into the dressing room. He emerged in a moment, screaming with terror—having encountered Gene in full costume, wearing his particularly hideous mask.

Gene delivered his speech, croaking and trembling, before an audience of roughly fifteen parents and other ranch people. At the opening of Scene One, the curtain swung open on a rebellious Billy, who self-consciously "said his piece" during the goblin scene. The goblins were the least inhibited of anyone, and did themselves proud, hopping off the stage with wonderful screeches and yowls when the time came for them to exit.

Scene Two took place in another part of the woods, about midnight. The curtain went up to show an old witch sitting cross legged in front of the orange fire, stirring a big iron pot. Freddie, having just escaped from the goblins, entered:

> Witch: So you ran away from home, did you? (*Sneering*)
> Freddie: Yes I did. I hope I never see them again.
> Witch: Do you want to come to our party?
> Freddie: I don't care.
> Witch: We need a nasty little boy to finish the recipe.
> Freddie: What kind of a recipe?
> Witch: We are going to turn all the bad boys into toads. We
> need one dead one first for the magic stew.
> [At this, the audience had its first real laugh.]
> Freddie: Uh-uh, not me!
> Witch: Yes you. You are the naughtiest boy I ever saw.
> Freddie: Why?
> Witch: You wouldn't go to bed, you wouldn't mind, and you
> lost your temper and tried to tear down the house.
> Freddie: How do YOU know?
> Witch: I've watched you and heard you lots of times. You had
> your chance to be good. It's all over now.
> Freddie: No!
> Witch: Come here, Freddie Smith!
> Freddie: NO! NO!
> Witch: Come here, Freddie Smith! (*She gets up and lurches
> toward him. He runs off stage as she falls.*)
> > CURTAIN

Scene Three
(*Scene: Another part of the woods, about midnight. Enter Freddy,
frightened and mussed up. He is very tired and he has gone through a lot
for one evening. He leans against a tree and wipes his forehead.*)

> Freddie: Gosh I wish I'd never left home.
> (*Enter ghost, who lays hand on Freddie's shoulder. Freddie is*

almost too tired to care.)

Freddie: Who are you?

Ghost: I am the ghost of an old man who was never happy.

Freddie: Why not?

Ghost: It's a long story. I was a bad boy once and ran away from home, and the things that happened to me may happen to you.

Freddie: What happened to you?

Ghost: I never had enough to eat. I was hungry and tired so I stole from people. I died a terrible death, and I have *never* been able to rest, not even in my grave.

Freddie: How long ago?

Ghost: Many years. So long ago I can't even remember. Go home, Freddie Smith! Go home while there is still time.

Freddie: I wonder if I can?

Ghost: There's still time if you go now. But remember—the witch is always waiting.

Freddie: Thank you—I'll go.

Ghost: You'd better *hurry*! Here come the goblins and the witch now!

All (*offstage*):

Go home, Freddie, while you can

Or you'll be a hop toad man

Bad boys come to no good end,

Go home now so your ways can mend!

(*Procession enters, headed by witch, followed by goblins, all making ghoulish gestures and chanting together. They circle around Freddie, and Ghost joins at the tail end. Witch leads them off stage.*)

Freddie (*to audience*): And so from now on I am a good boy and live happily ever after.

CURTAIN

The curtain rang shut as the last ghoul disappeared behind its scanty folds.

I plastered cold cream all over small wrinkled masculine faces to take off the chalk makeup we had so enthusiastically applied, while outside the scraping of furniture told of preparation for the dance. Desks were shoved up as close to the walls as possible, leaving a full width of fourteen feet to be danced across. Lengthwise, with the curtain down, we managed to squeeze out almost twenty. It was not the place for a Viennese waltz, exactly, nor for the ground-eating schottische performed so beautifully by Mr. and Mrs. Hirsch—when they had room to turn around in. Neither was the music superlative, as it was supplied by a pile of 45 RPM records that had sat on a hot shelf for two winters and undergone certain melodic alterations as a result.

The spirit of our gathering, however, was not to be daunted by such trivia. Frequent trips outdoors by gentleman members, along with a certain alcoholic fragrance that drifted above our heads, seemed to increase a general sense of well-being. Couples who hung back shyly from the dance floor were soon entangled with the rest of the perspiring crowd, which seemed larger than it was. And Doc, as the evening wore on, began to assume the spotlight. With their legs and arms flailing like unrelated windmills, he and his partner—whoever she happened to be—would careen about the floor knocking all obstructions to the sidelines, Doc red with exertion, and frequently bursting into song:

> Oh, I'm goin' home in a little red wagon,
> I'm goin' home just a-pukin' and a-gaggin' . . .

Doc was finally rescued from his wagon by a call to the most liberal feed our schoolhouse had ever produced. The children were summoned in from their hysterical romping in the dark; Gene deserted his post as record-changer; tiny ones collapsed in sleep on my floor were gathered up and offered a piece of cake before they went home. Only the baby asleep on my bed went unrefreshed by the plentiful supply of sandwiches, pickles, cake, and steaming coffee. Full, and reasonably contented, the cast members and audience pulled out for home.

Next morning, scattered across a muddy schoolyard, I beheld the shattered remnants of five or six pumpkins—and the empty bottles of four hefty fifths of whisky. Along the edge of the girls' toilet, concealed by some grass, lay another—one-third full.

Billy had found it underneath a car whose owner shall be nameless, and had hidden it.

CHAPTER FIVE

We Are the Girls from the Institute

We were hard at work one day when a strange car drove up outside the schoolhouse. I viewed the schoolroom in panic, fairly sure the visitor was some kind of inspector. Our slop pail was full of dirty water from the aquarium, which Billy had just cleaned, and wet paper towels had not all hit their mark in the trash basket. Moreover, the desks were entirely covered with piles of books we were sorting and reshelving according to a new library system.

In short, we were not clad in our Sunday best. I stifled an impulse to flee from the insistent rapping at our front door but instead pulled it open with all possible dignity. Outside stood a dark-haired young man.

"Hello," he said. "I'm the county sanitarian."

I shot a panicky glance around our unsanitary room while he explained that he had come out to check our water supply and other devices, including the toilets. He would just walk around outside if that was all right, taking samples and checking what he came to inspect.

"Fine," I said. "Let me know if you need any help." As soon as he had vanished outdoors we did a quick pick-up around the room. Suspicion among the children was great over "that stranger snoopin' around out there," and they could not keep their minds on their work at all.

At last the sanitarian reappeared, beckoning me outdoors to inspect the well with him.

"I don't think it is contaminated," he said, "but the way dirty water can leak in around the top here isn't so good. Even if we get a clear test on it, it may still get polluted at any time. I'll send you plans showing how it can be fixed—and a set of plans showing how to raise the innards of the pump and how to block the entrance of outside water.

"The toilets are all right but they should be painted. And make sure the children leave those lids down or flies will be everywhere—they fly right up out of those pits and land first thing on somebody's sandwich. I'll have your water test results back as soon as I can."

"Thanks a lot," I said—much relieved that he hadn't found anything more serious. "Is there anything else that should be done?"

"Yes, there is," he replied. "As a matter of fact that's why I came out here so early. There's a dance in Miles City a week from Saturday with a big-name band. How about coming along?"

I was nothing short of astonished. I went to the dance with him, to the huge entertainment of the neighbors. And before long we had a clear test on the water from the state laboratory!

The sanitarian in fact had a lasting effect on school organization. We had instigated a system of cleanup jobs the first day, and each child had his or her own particular beat to patrol before going-home time. Dick emptied the trash baskets; Gary and Eddie picked up scraps of paper from the floor and sprinkled sweeping compound; Pansy erased the blackboards and beat the erasers; Bill tidied the science table and fed its inhabitants; Leslie straightened up the porch; and Gene carried water and did other heavier tasks as need demanded. With the advent of the sanitarian, we established a new job by that title. Our own sanitarian had to empty the slop pail and be sure that the washstand was wiped and tidy before we went home.

For the toilets, in light of the sanitarian's recommendations, we designed and executed a pair of lurid posters on old white shirt cardboards. The girls' poster showed a privy with its lid open, disgorging a swarm of large black flies. The boys' poster showed a man taking a bite out of a ham sandwich, on which sat a large and obviously germ-ridden fly. "Keep It Down" and "Keep the Lid On" read the crayoned mottos.

The posters seemed to help. In fact, to one used to modern plumbing, it is surprising how clean and pleasant an outdoor toilet can be. This revelation applies to other areas as well. The first day or two without modern conveniences, one tends to grumble and feel demoted to the dark ages. After that, the rituals of carrying water and coal, of lighting gas or kerosene lamps, or of heating dishwater become customary and provide a pleasant sense of independence. And the glow from lamps, yellow and golden, sheds a far warmer circle of light than the balding glare from electric overheads. There is a certain beauty of movement in lifting a dipper of cool water from a sparkling porcelain pail. Stepping outdoors can bring one very close to stars and storms or to the faint pulsing touches of a spring night wind.

Anyone doing things the old-fashioned way grabs at the chance to modernize when possible. But in the meantime the lamplight is very beautiful. I knew a young Wellesley graduate who married a cowboy and lived with him in a camp eleven miles up an often impassible road, and who raised three very attractive babies without complaining, with hand-carried water, an old coal stove, a gasoline-powered washing machine, and no electricity.

>f

In mid-October our first report cards were due, and the job of filling them out seemed fraught with peril. These seven children were the only students I had ever taught. Would work that seemed excellent to me stand up with work from a town school? Was Eddie—so much the quickest in our first grade—really advanced for his age, or were the others only slow? Gene was certainly not up to seventh-grade standards in any subject. In fact, Billy and Gene both seemed so far behind that I had given them a complete set of metropolitan tests a week before, so that I could analyze what grade levels they were actually working at. Billy turned out to be below average and Gene was drastically behind, rating a fourth-grade level in reading, which of course crippled all his other work. But who would I be to march in and start failing Gene? Other teachers, who must have known what they were doing, had passed him in previous years. It was all very perplexing.

Resolutely, I sat down at my desk and pulled out the blank report cards, along with all available records on each child's work. The cards provided space for rankings on health, conduct, and attendance reports, as well as for a short note from the teacher. There were also "cubbyholes" for grades in sixteen different subjects: arithmetic, arts, civics, geography, handwriting, history, health, language, physical education, music, reading, science, spelling, citizenship habits, health habits, and study habits.

I groaned. And proceeded to spend three long evenings comparing the work of one child with another, in consultation with the teacher's manual, which failed to help. At last I arranged a set of grades for each child. Next came what seemed to be the most sensible section of the reports—the individual notes to parents.

The children's characteristics were all familiar by now—Gene's lethargy, Billy's antagonism, Dick's wild imagination. I'd visited all their homes, loping down the road of an evening on good gray Annie, who stood patiently by each home, tied outside, for two or three hours while supper was eaten and the dishes washed. Children behaved differently at home! Pansy, so controlled and ladylike in the classroom, could scream like a banshee in the company of her younger brothers and sister; Leslie, always grown up and cooperative in school, was forever showing off to his parents by exhibitions of "badness"—rubbing his mother's hand lotion all over his head or covering his face with lipstick and rouge. Gary, our littlest, had three smaller brothers and sisters, in addition to the older Dick, whom he bossed pitilessly in order to feel big for once. And Billy turned into a spitting little hellion around his stepmother, swearing at her and issuing the most appalling threats as soon as his father left the house.

At school we had worked into a fairly harmonious little family—with bad days of course, but generally improving. The room, untidy during the day, became respectable, thanks to our cleanup duties, by the time the children went home. I rarely had to remind the children to do their jobs. The little bits of badness—talking back, or pinching, or sulkiness—had become easy to respond to through a frown or a wink or a tease:

"Why Dick," I'd say, "your lower lip is out so far you'll trip on it."

Dick's scowl would strive mightily, and then vanish beneath an overpowering grin.

"Gene," I would say when he was obviously wasting time, "let's quit the fiddle-faddle and get moving."

Sometimes Gene was resentful, but more often than not, he was a pretty good sport.

The question was how to tell parents what their children were accomplishing. It must be done with understanding and tact, and the undercurrent of belief in each child that would override any needed criticism. Report cards were important to parents, I thought. But how could even a teacher know who deserved an arbitrary A or B? If a child had tried his utmost, that should be recorded and explained—even if his work was still sadly below standard. If his previous failures had discouraged him, there was greater success in his turning the tide and becoming eager to learn again, than in any measurable mastery of fact or skill. Such intangible results were impossible to write, though, into the B's and C's and D's that could carry a shattering impact at home. His father would scold him, certainly—maybe punish him by denying a new toy or a trip to town. The bad report cards would make him hate school worse than ever, and his few slow gains would be negated.

Take Billy, for instance. Too cheerful a report would be a bald lie. Too critical a one would bring the heavens down on him at home, especially when his lower grades were compared to Eddie's A's. I worried and wondered, and at last wrote the following note:

> Bill is behind his grade in reading, which explains his low mark
> (D+) for this report. He is improving fast in many areas of work.
> As soon as he learns to pull with the team a little more, he will
> have a better time in school. Somehow he started this year with a
> feeling that things were against him, but he is working out of this
> and already his attitude is improving. Bill does well in arithmetic
> and science. A little more cooperation, and the rest of his report
> will fall in line.

The reports went home the next day, and sure enough there followed a scene of violence in Bill's home. He was rebellion itself for the next week, and the rest of us had to simply grit our teeth and endure him. Bill's case was one of painfully slow progress and frequent sharp setbacks, which one had to take in stride. But there was comfort in the fact that his report had erred, if anywhere, on the side of mercy.

At the end of October we had our first school holiday so that I could attend a "Teacher's Institute" and State Conference held for three days in Miles City. The Institute would take place on the first day and the Conference would follow on the second and third days. I had never been to an Institute and thought irreverently of an old rhyme as I approached town:

Aroodiddy toot, aroodiddy toot!
We are the girls from the Institute.
We don't smoke and we don't chew,
And we don't go with the boys who do.

The Institute turned out to be a meeting held for all the rural teachers in our county, which stretched forty miles across the state and fifty miles from end to end. Back on the gravel roads among the sagebrush-dotted hills, there were about twenty one-teacher schools. We met in the banquet room of a large town café.

Fascinated, I looked about me. Seated along both sides of the long table were people of all descriptions, men and women, young and old. Across the way was a smiling, black-haired girl, the teacher of the Garland School. On the left was a heavyset man with glasses. A handsome white-haired couple—man and wife—sat together beyond him, next to a little old lady whose snapping eyes and soft gray hair gave her an expression of lively kindliness. Another young girl sat on the right, and beyond her a thin young man with an undershot chin and heavy glasses. A stranger entering the room might have guessed the identity of this group to be almost anything—a club, a political group, a church gathering. It certainly did not have the obvious marks of a teachers' meeting.

At the head of our table sat Mrs. Richardson, the motherly county superintendent who had lent so many books and supplies for the opening of the SH School. It was nice to see her again. Several times in the past few weeks she had put aside her work to talk over teaching problems with me when I arrived somewhat woebegone from the country. Her suggestions and, above all, her friendly support, were a great boon on days when doubting parents made me wonder if I was on the wrong track.

"You know," Mrs. Richardson told me, her eyes twinkling, "When I began to teach, my supervisor thought I was just *awful*. I let the children move around a lot, and when they finished their regular work, if they wanted to read on the floor, why that was fine with me. So glad I was to have them volunteering to read at all—why not on the floor? And then one day the supervisor came out for a visit and there they all were. She had a fit."

I told her of the local gossip that had begun when Timber started helping me work on the shed at night.

"Oh, pooh," she said. "Trouble with a lot of people is they've forgotten what it is to be young."

Mrs. Richardson was one of the people who would never forget that.

After she called the meeting to order, each of us stood up in turn to introduce ourselves and briefly describe our schools. As teacher after teacher spoke out, I began to realize the scope of educational problems in the area where the population was too thin to support specialized institutions. The heavy-set gentleman with glasses had only four children in his school, but one of them—in the fourth grade—was a twenty-year-old girl who was completely blind. He was teaching her to read Braille, preparing materials for her on a special typewriter—and doing his best to stay a step or two ahead of her, translating stories from a regular fourth-grade reader!

Miss Miller—of the Garland School—had among her four students a mentally handicapped boy, ten years old, who had never been to school. From an underprivileged family, life had held little for him until she arrived. His speech was crippled and his mind at the age of a five-year-old. She was working with him patiently on a pre-Kindergarten level, and already his little face turned up to her with pathetic devotion.

The lively little gray-haired lady was preparing to run a sort of boarding school when the weather closed in and blizzards made it dangerous for her six pupils to walk or ride home. She had laid in a stock of extra food, and bedding had been brought from home. If the weather got bad, the children would just stay with her at the school, several nights perhaps, until it cleared enough for them to get home safely.

At one point in our meeting, when Mrs. Richardson was giving us directions for the observation of Pioneer Day, she got proudly to her feet.

"I believe," she said, "that I am one of the pioneers." Her parents had come to the country in a prairie schooner.

The teachers went on to tell more stories. The white-haired couple, exuding an air of ease and authority, presided at the county's only consolidated school (formed by merging discontinued smaller schools), located in a somewhat lawless wheat-growing district north of town. This was a place where, on Halloween, privies were hoisted up flagpoles and bridges torn out as a merry joke on the trucks and cars that consequently crashed into the ditch. The attitude of the school's students was tough when the Dentons moved out there.

The Dentons had not been there long before they were annoyed by a rash of obscene scrawlings on the schoolhouse walls and on a street near the school building. This sort of thing apparently happened so regularly that local people were fairly resigned to it. Not Mr. Denton, who held the post of principal.

The schoolchildren, many of whom were seventh- and eighth-graders, were unusually fond of athletic contests and games—and had some crack players lined up for the coming season. Mr. Denton let all preparation and training go forward. Then one day he announced that until the authors of certain new phrases on the walls came to him and confessed, all further athletics would be canceled.

The culprits could come to him privately at any hour of the day or night, he said. But each would kindly bring his father.

For a week the suspense mounted, as the date of the opening game drew near. Nothing more was said on the subject. No more obscene words were noticed. And still, apparently, nobody had had the courage to confess.

At the eleventh hour, an announcement came down from the office that the matter had been taken care of. The game was on. Whoever had gone to the Denton house with his father in the dead of night was never revealed. But no more repetitions occurred.

I began to respect the Dentons as people of some ability.

At the Institute we discussed the realistic program that the State of Montana had developed for its small country schools, where, as one booklet read, "The inconveniences of frontier life still exist." Such schools as ours had obvious disadvantages in terms of limited enrollment and scarcity of supplies with which to work. But the state program hoped to show that a good teacher could turn these into advantages if she rose to the challenge.

Limited enrollment in rural schools meant that the teacher could provide a degree of individual attention to her children, which was impossible in town. She could build a program entirely suited to each child's needs and have time to carry it out—in the finest educational manner. The limited school resources imposed by small budgets could be seen as a marvelous chance to create and supply, together with the children, the things most needed. Such creative endeavors built a type of resourceful citizenship that town schools had difficulty matching. Which child was really getting the better education—the one who walked into a beautifully equipped room or the one who had planned and struggled and discussed and written letters and voted and gone shopping himself for the few things his school possessed?

We talked about such things. To increase consciousness of what a country school should be, Montana had drawn up an exhaustive set of standards in the form of a five-year evaluation program. Each school board and teacher had copies of a booklet outlining these standards and were charged with evaluating their own school plant on a point system once a year. If in any of eight categories, such as Equipment, Library, Building or Grounds, they fell below a minimum number of points, the school would no longer be certified by the state, its money cut off.

We explored the evaluation booklets during the Institute, seeing what last year's criticisms of our schools had been. For the SH, improvements listed as necessary had included storm windows, a flag pole, an encyclopedia, a fence, a globe, and a fire extinguisher. No mention had been made of a stove for the teacher or books for our mouse-chewed library. I wondered mildly if the evaluation plan was at fault, or merely the evaluators, whoever they were.

At our "No Host Luncheon," I met, at last, the teacher from up the road on Star Creek—the one who taught Aunt Betty's kids. I banished my former homicidal impulses toward her, or at least concealed them, and courteously inquired about her methods of teaching reading.

"Oh, I go by what they taught us in school," she said with a wry smile, and a quick calculation revealed that she must have been in school about 1930. "We teach them action words first, like "run" or "skip" or "hop"—and they associate the word with doing what it says.

Mine have come along nice and quick; they've gone through two little books already." This in an offhand tone. "There's nothing to it, once you get onto it."

I neglected to inform her how many little books the SH first graders had gone through: none. Doubtless she knew anyway.

Another teacher, vintage about 1910, chimed in. "Well I teach mine the alphabet first," she said, "and spelling right along with the whole shebang. Every word they can read, they can spell it too."

That was a system I happened to know (dating back to the Roman Empire). Current educators scorned it.

"I teach them by phonics," said a third. "They learn the letter sounds first and then they sound out their new words. We give them lots of word families too, like 'ball, call, wall, hall.'"

No wonder there was such confusion about teaching reading, with methods from the last five or six decades all in use at once. In these gloriously independent country schools, teachers of all ages could do pretty much as they pleased. I had been taught, however, that understanding was the thing to emphasize, not the arrangement of letters or a series of meaningless word families. Children could recognize by sight whole words like "mother" and "dog" and "Jerry" without any dissection process. The main thing at first was to get them interested in stories and books and liking what they found in them. The finer skills of reading would come later.

But heaven knows I was no authority. And Betty's kids had gone through two little books.

The Institute, with its twenty-two teachers, was a strictly home-county, family affair. The next two days were devoted to a large whoop-de-do conference of the Montana Education Association (MEA), drawing school people from the entire eastern half of the state. Commentary at local bars was rampant as hundreds of teachers flocked into town.

"Where you been, Joe?" asked the proprietor of one establishment.

"Out on the steps of The Olive," said Joe, "watching all them legs go by."

"I had to sleep in a hotel full of those damn teachers one time," recalled the bartender. "Worse than a Shriners' convention! They were drunk as ticks, screaming and yelling all night long, carrying each other up and down the halls 'cause half of them couldn't even walk."

"How do you know?"

"Hell, they kept me awake all night. Stay away from a drunken schoolmarm."

A fat membership fee was charged to attend the big MEA convention, a fact not mentioned in the preliminary announcement. Annoyed by that omission, I was more annoyed to learn that our chief speakers would give talks on the newspaper business and the economics of an oil basin, when we had come to learn about teaching! The whole thing seemed nonsensical, but it was too late to go back to the country and hold school. When a few familiar faces drifted past in the milling crowd, I hastened to join them. One was the pioneer lady; her companion was the teacher of reading by the alphabetic method. Together the three of us pushed our way into the back row of a crowded classroom, where one of the workshop sessions was under way.

". . . They have risen nobly to the challenge," the speaker was saying, "and have done their part like noble war horses at the call to battle. We cannot praise them enough. But now it is time for them to go on to greener pastures, and to let younger women—women who are professionally *capable* of the great job of teacher—take their places in the schools which are second to none in the role of making Montana great."

I looked questioningly at my companions, whose gray hackles were beginning to rise. Old war horses, were they?

"These older teachers," the man continued, "are badly out of date in a world that asks, nay, demands the modern approach. Many of them have never even gone to a teachers college. Many were certified in days when a college education was not necessary to teach school. Today they are filling a gap which, to be sure, we are grateful for; but the gap must be better filled if our children are not to suffer. These women cannot give them the education they deserve.

"We need professionally trained teachers, teachers who have had modern courses in college, teachers who can meet the demands of the day from their background of training in modern education. I ask you, ladies, to join in this movement for higher teaching standards; I ask you to band together in this organization and to give your support to measures by which we may achieve this great end."

The speaker sat down. Gone was my annoyance at ancient methods of teaching reading, replaced by a surge of sympathy for the old war horses who were getting so merrily shoved aside. I got to my feet.

"I don't completely agree with you," I said. "For one thing, a lot of these older teachers have years of experience which have taught them a great deal. And for another thing, I'm not sure that teachers colleges do the best job of training teachers because I just graduated from a university where they were finding out differently."

The speaker looked up in surprise.

"You can't work with children for thirty years," interjected one of my companions indignantly, "and not know *something*. You fellers are just tickled to death to get us older women in here and grab our membership fees and then try to argue us out of a job."

There was a murmur of consent through the room. The speaker, who had been trying to pass a resolution favoring higher standards of teaching, found himself backed against a wall.

"At my college," I continued, "they were wondering if four years of methods in a teachers college turns out the best teachers anyway. They were finding out that such people know lots of teaching methods, but they don't know any subjects to teach, like history or science or literature. All they know are methods. If a girl goes to college, she might as well take plenty of subject matter and pick up teaching tricks on the side or in her last year."

"All those college girls do is get married anyway," said someone sourly.

A pert-faced little nun from a nearby mission to the Indians spoke next. "Well," she said briskly, "of course *we* don't have *that* problem. But we find that professional training is a very useful thing."

"It's plenty useful in its place," spoke out another woman. "But it's not the whole story. A teacher needs tricks of the trade, but she also has to love children and know something besides—I mean, some subject matter of her own."

"If you love the kids and have some good common sense, you can teach just fine," neighed one of the war horses.

"May I ask where you went to college?" the speaker addressed me suspiciously.

"To Cornell University, sir."

"And what did you major in?"

"Agriculture."

"And how on earth did you become a teacher?"

"I took a great many courses in liberal arts along with my agriculture work, and finished with a summer session of teacher's training after graduation."

"So all the teacher's training you have had is one summer session?"

"Yes, sir. And to tell the truth I learned more from books read on my own than I did from courses."

"Well!"

"It would seem," commented someone mildly, "that a good deal depends on the human element, which is rather hard to standardize."

In despair the speaker saw his resolution to outlaw old teachers slipping down the drain as the period ended. To a degree he had been right; more and better teachers *were* badly needed. But was a certain number of hours in education training a guarantee of better teachers? Some of the worst old dictatorial diehards had been trained to the teeth!

I felt good as we walked out. Might be a war horse myself some day! One never knew where the teaching profession might lead. And the "normal schools" had little to offer in times like ours.

In truth, it would have taken an abnormal graduate of any "normal school" to cope with the situations that cropped up so frequently in a typical rural school. For instance, there was the case of Mrs. Wiggins, a teacher at the Beckton School in Wyoming, where I was myself a student in the fourth grade. In that sixteen-child, eight-grade school, Mrs. Wiggins found her hands very full indeed, especially since she had just moved from a one-grade teaching position in Missouri. The transition was taxing, and this particular school especially taxing because of a family of seven cross-eyed children, the offspring of a migratory sugar beet worker, several of whom were in attendance. Oldest and wisest of the lot was Lester, who got his share of the switchings Mrs. Wiggins soon learned to dole out.

It was a peaceful autumn day when Lester pulled off his most daring revolt. For a minor misbehavior, he had been shut up, during recess, in the school library—a small closet-sized room equipped with bookshelves, which Mrs. Wiggins had spent much recent labor in arranging. The books were now catalogued and alphabetized on the shelves. When recess was over, classes resumed. For the moment nobody remembered Lester.

Then, into the silence, burst a deafening staccato uproar, echoing directly above the ceiling. "Thump a boom, BANG BANG!" The noises repeated a time or two, then stilled a moment—only to resume as Mrs. Wiggins rushed into the library, switch in hand.

Lester had vanished. Piles of books lay in jumbled heaps on the floor. And muddy boot prints trailed up the emptied shelves all the way to the attic cubbyhole through which Lester had plainly escaped.

"Come down!" commanded Mrs. Wiggins, brandishing the switch. But Lester had no such intention. "Thump a boom BANG!" drummed his heels above the heads of an enthralled audience. "Thumpety BANG bang BANG!"

And in the attic Lester remained for the rest of the school day. How scores were finally settled I do not know, but a truce was declared the following day. Mrs. Wiggins did not switch him again, and his general conduct was mysteriously improved—maybe by the attic's rarified air.

In bygone years children had been bold enough to lock their hapless teacher in the schoolhouse when she attempted to keep them after school. But today's teachers, like Mrs. Wiggins, still had their problems, often living by themselves and forced to fall back on their own resources. Particularly interesting were schools located on Indian reservations, where there was little danger but sometimes a touch of suspense. One young mother, living alone with her children on the edge of a small town on the Cheyenne reservation, was made nervous by a recent series of housebreakings. A neighbor had been alarmed one evening when a stranger had crawled into bed with her after cutting a neat, round hole in the screen door to let himself in. Her shrieks drove him rapidly away, muttering that it must have been the wrong house.

But the matter had upset the community, including the young mother whose unease increased after this incident.

Suddenly the local teacher's phone began ringing furiously in the dead of night.

"It's the Indians," sobbed the young mother. "They've been in the bushes around the house all evening, and I don't dare go for help because of leaving the children."

The teacher, a stalwart individual, jerked a pair of overalls on over her nightgown and set forth on foot to the house some distance away. There she found two young Cheyennes, very drunk, giggling as they leaned down to peer under the window shades.

"Now GET OUT!" roared the teacher, slamming the nearest one hard with the heel of her bedroom slipper, "and DON'T EVER COME BACK!"

The intruders fled, and the teacher marched back to bed.

Despite their often lonely quarters, country teachers are usually not of a disposition to be bothered by solitude. But once in a while, the situation can get overpowering even for them. Such was the case of Miss Johnson, whom I had met on the train. Accepting a school as a substitute in the dead of winter, she had known little of what to expect upon arriving at a small Dakota town. All she knew was that the other teacher was gone, and a replacement was needed badly to finish out the year.

She was taken from town out to the schoolhouse in the midst of a blizzard. There she heard an appalling tale. The previous teacher had been shot to death two weeks before, in that very schoolhouse, by a crazed lover who afterward shot himself. Terrified, the children—who had witnessed the murder—had run home to tell their parents.

Both bodies were recovered from the blood-soaked teacherage where the new teacher had to live. Scrubbed and painted, it still held an air of horror. And bound to her contract, the new teacher stuck it out to the end of the school term, remembering for the rest of her life the hours she spent listening to the shrieking wind at night, staring at the bullet holes in the wall and floor.

CHAPTER SIX

Country School Christmas

We began to get ready for Christmas before Thanksgiving. Then along came the old clothes drive to link up the two holidays and make life a little more hectic. The fundraiser was for overseas relief, benefiting refugee children. A great paper sack came out from town, with enough brochures sufficient for a school twenty times our size, telling parents that outgrown clothes could make some foreign child warm again, and asking for the sake of children everywhere a small offering, an outgrown sweater, socks, anything against the cold.

There was a picture, too, of a thin little dark-haired girl asleep in a pile of rags in some cold, distant city. It was a real photograph of a real little girl, her dark-lashed eyes closed peacefully in her drawn little face—a little girl of the kind Pansy longed for here in school, who had had tough luck and needed someone so badly to help her out, give her a hand.

The children took her right to heart and named her Caroline. For a time Caroline lived with us—her picture on the bulletin board, her thin face and tattered clothes in everyone's mind. Pansy and Billy made up little stories about her during English period. Pansy wrote a few sentences in her usual neat hand, but Billy for once outdid her—in thought if not in execution.

"Caroline is a little girl had No clothes She is very poor she is a little girl far across the sea," he wrote. "She lives very poor. I suppose she would like to live in America because she is poor she has No clothes. If we get a chance we will send you some clothes. If you get a chance send us a letter."

Afterward Billy asked many questions about people overseas and why they were poor. I reminded all the children about war movies they had seen and what a mess things were after a lot of fighting had taken place.

"How would you like to live where all that fighting went on?" I asked, and their eyes were wide with concern. "Think what your house might be like if a bomb hit it or a shell from one of those big guns. Where would all your clothes and toys be then?"

"I guess they wouldn't be no place," said Billy.

"Other things could happen too," I explained. "Maybe your mom and dad might be killed. Maybe you'd have nowhere to go, and be cold and hungry and all alone. That's what happened to children like Caroline."

"Or get killed your own self!" said Dick.

"Did kids get killed in the war, Miss Margot?" asked Pansy.

"Yes, some of them did. But the ones we want to think about are the alive ones that we can help. Any old clothes you have at home will make them very happy. It's like a Christmas present for someone you don't know."

In a day or two the clothes began to come in. Bundles and bundles of clothes, nice things, including from the Wells family, whose own five children stood in line for hand-me-downs, and the Hirsches, whose four did as well. From Gene came a few things, and even some men at the ranch made donations. Only Billy and Eddie, who had been so interested, brought nothing. Billy was obviously troubled about it, so I said nothing.

Later I learned that his father had been adamant in his opposition. "Any old clothes we got are going to good honest-to-God Americans," he had said. "None of them damned Europeans."

Plainly what a child learned in school could be easily nullified by a disapproving papa.

A newcomer arrived at school in the midst of the old clothes drive. One morning, a month earlier, Dick and Gary had rushed into the schoolhouse, crying breathlessly, "Poochie's had she pups! Poochie's had she pups! Eight pups, Poochie's had!"

Poochie was a warm-coated and warmhearted border collie, as good with children as any of her forbears had been with sheep. And she'd had the pups now!

"There's eight," said Gary wonderingly.

"Papa says we got to drownded 'em," said Dick sadly. "All except one or two maybe. Gee they're little."

"Well," I said, "you tell your papa to keep one more and I'll take him." A dog in the schoolhouse was just what it needed. We had two kittens, who got along all right, but they were poor company. A dog would be better.

"We's feedin' Poochie lots of milk," continued Gary. "We give Poochie the milk and then it runs out she teats and the pups gets it!"

We laughed at him. He was so serious and so amazed.

A month later, before Christmas, the boys' mother came in one afternoon bearing the new puppy. He was a good-sized little dog by then, soft and black and white, with pointed ears that fell over his eyes in a piglike manner. In fact, with his rolls of puppy pudginess, he was rather piglike all over, except for his lengthy tail, which stuck straight up and was white tipped like the tail of a silver fox. The black markings on his short coat gave him a funny appearance from the rear, resembling a pair of breeches just about to slip off. I named him Shorty.

Many times in the next months Shorty could have used real breeches. Puddles appeared in a great variety of places. Under my bed, in the library corner, by the science table, beneath the first grade desks—each morning brought its share of surprises to clean up before the children arrived. Also, things began to be missing from the children's lockers. Eddie's mitten would vanish, to turn up later under the bookshelf or stove; or Pansy's scarf would go missing altogether. Daily, a hideous caterwauling would disrupt some recitation, and lessons would cease while I rushed to rescue one of the kittens from too-vigorous puppy play.

"Shorty, let go!" I would command and lift the kitten from his jaws. A moment later the kitten would be purring and rubbing against him, asking for more.

The children greatly enjoyed our problems in animal discipline. My gray mare Annie would have to be shooed away repeatedly from the middle of playground games. So did the puppy. The kittens had to be discouraged from fishing in the goldfish aquarium and from hurtling across the floor in wild games during school hours. Often they crawled inside the glass cupboard door, to sit purring on our piled supply of paper. Shorty, when he couldn't manhandle a kitten, chewed up every stray crayon that rolled his way, resulting in a remarkable improvement in classroom neatness. And he often chose to park himself at the feet of some allegedly studying child to tug on his shoelaces.

But there was no shutting him out. The kittens would be bodily removed from Gene's shoulder, where they were fond of lingering, and carried into the teacherage if they insisted on playing with someone's pencil as he wrote. Not so Shorty, who wailed and howled in outrage when the door was closed on him. During some classes I held him on my lap to keep him still; at other times he collapsed in sleep under my desk. At any rate, we were following the teacher's manual, which recommended a classroom pet or two!

The Yuletide season had found a good beginning in the children's concern for Caroline. Their reaction to her picture was a pleasant surprise; a generous and big-hearted spirit had come to life, even in the littlest ones, a quality that one might not think children could possess. This quality must be kept as a foundation for whatever performance we came up with at Christmas. It was, traditionally, the most important program of the year.

Last year's program in the school had been limited, since there had only been three children. They had recited poems for the better part of it, and were followed by the appearance of a singular Santa Claus. Nobody had been able to obtain a red Santa suit, however. Nothing daunted, Santa had come anyhow—in a mask and a bearskin coat, looking more like a Yukon highway robber than a jovial St. Nick. The children in the audience, particularly four- and five-year-old preschoolers, had shrieked in terror. After much motherly cajoling, and with the help of the oranges that this strange monster had distributed around the room, they were mollified. But from then on they regarded Santa Claus as somewhat of a fearful deceiver. I knew I had to set this to rights by getting a real Santa Claus suit even if it meant assaulting some city bell ringer. We also needed a program that would offer more to all concerned than childish lisping of "I Want a Little Dolly."

So together we wrote a play woven, not around tinselly new toys, but around the old story of Christmas that so few of the children had heard. It featured Mary and Joseph and the baby, and the innkeeper and the shepherds. And it had children who came with the shepherds, to see the baby Jesus on Christmas morning. I wanted the play to center around the children, an outgrowth of the lovely old poem by Eugene Field:

> Why do bells for Christmas ring?
> Why do little children sing?
>
> Once a lovely, shining star,
> Seen by shepherds from afar
> Gently moved until its light
> Made a manger's cradle bright.
>
> There a darling baby lay,
> Pillowed soft upon the hay,
> And his mother sang and smiled,
> "This is Christ, the holy child."
>
> So the bells for Christmas ring
> So the little children sing.

As the play began, our own "little children" would recite these verses together, softly and clearly, as a carol without music.

Pansy, of course, was Mary. Gene was Joseph. Billy, charged with responsibility, was the innkeeper. And the first-graders were children and shepherds. Our rehearsals were lessons in more than speech and diction. Question after question came up about Christmas and Mary and God. Sometimes we had to stop everything until some sort of an answer was found to satisfy the wide little eyes. This happened one day during a first-grade rehearsal, while the older children were working on their lessons, but of course listening in. The little children wanted to know what happened when the baby Jesus grew up. Unversed in Bible teaching, I simply told them the elements of the whole story.

"He grew up to be a good man who did wonderful things for people everywhere," I explained.

"And then what?"

"Then some of the people thought he was a bad man instead of a good one. So they killed him."

"How?" asked Eddie, with a troubled expression. Eddie had lost his usual glee at the prospect of bloodshed.

"On the cross," announced Leslie. "We got one on the wall in our house, shows all about it. Waynie busted the end off it, though. They nailed him."

"They nailed *Waynie*?"

"No. God."

"No, they never," contradicted Pansy from her seat, even though she was supposed to be working. "Father Pat told Mama they *crucified* him on that cross."

"And that was where he died," I finished. "But you know something wonderful happened after that. Because he came back to life again, just as if he had never been dead at all. And he stayed around for a few days, and said goodbye to his friends, and then he went straight up to heaven."

There was an incredulous pause.

"How could he come alive that way?" asked Eddie, full of skepticism. "When you're dead you're dead, like an old cow."

"And you rot," supplied Gary, "and worms gets you."

"Well the worms never got Jesus," I said. "You see he never really died. Nobody could ever really kill him, not for keeps. He went up to heaven and he's still alive now."

"Right *now*?"

"Yes."

"Is he coming back?"

"Some people say he is," I answered, not knowing quite what to say. "But I don't think anybody knows for sure."

"Maybe he'll come to the Christmas play and bring Santa Claus," suggested Leslie.

"Well," I asked significantly, "would you want him to see the Christmas play the way it is right now?" Our rehearsals had been hectic—and some silliness had crept in.

"This ain't a funny play like that other one at Halloween, is it Miss Margot?" asked Billy from his seat. Billy, as usual, had been giggling and showing off.

"No it's not. How will it sound with a lot of big TEE HEE HEE's all through it?"

Billy returned to his third-grade reader.

Dick had been thinking long and hard. "I sure hope he doesn't step on a loose board up there like in our hay mow," he said. "I sure hope Jesus doesn't fall down here and get hurt. I sure wish he'd land some place soft like our straw stack, if he fell down here."

I tried to assure him that heaven was a pretty well-built place, and they kept the loose boards fixed there so nobody would fall through. For the moment there were no more questions, so we returned to our rehearsal of the first-grade scene, the concluding one. I read the older children's parts, and the first-graders practiced saying their own.

The scene portrayed Mary and Joseph leaning over the manger. Two shepherds, Leslie and Dick, were to rush in.

"We came as fast as we could," panted Leslie, "to worship the child." He had trouble with the word "worship." It always sounded like "wash up."

"Last night we heard singing," supplied Dick, "and seen the star," broke in Leslie.

"And then the angels came," finished Dick, "So many they filled the sky."

"Were you afraid?" I asked, for Mary.

"The angel said to fear not," answered Leslie.

"Merry Christmas, Mary and Joseph," chorused both shepherds. "Merry Christmas to the baby."

"Miss Margot?" It was Billy again. "Why would they be scared of the angels?"

"Well, Billy, if you went out tonight after it was dark—oh, about five o'clock—pretend you and Eddie went out to feed the chickens and bring in a bucket of coal. And suddenly you heard some beautiful singing, and you knew nobody left the radio on, and there wasn't anybody out in the hills to sing like that. But you heard it anyway, louder and louder, and bang! There was a big bright light and hundreds of angels with white wings flying around your head . . ."

"I'd jump out of my pants!" cried Dick.

We all laughed. "Well, the shepherds were scared too," I explained. "But then one of the angels said not to worry because this little baby had just been born and he was going to do a lot of good things for people. And the angels were just sort of having a party for him."

"Did those sheepherders just take right off to town?" asked Leslie.

"They went as fast as they could to see the baby."

"Horseback?" asked Gary, "or in the pickup?"

"No sir," said Leslie. "In them days they didn't have nothing to ride except angels."

Gene, the seventh-grader, and I grinned at the picture of shepherds winging through the sky angel-back.

"Come on, let's finish up," I directed. How *would* you explain an angel?

Three first-graders were to enter in tip-toed wonder to see the holy baby on Christmas morning. They were to play themselves, as completely as possible. The dialogue ran as follows:

> Gary: Is *that* the baby?
>
> Mary (*played by Pansy*): Yes, he is. The Little Lord Jesus.
>
> Dick: He looks like any old baby.
>
> Eddie: Well, he isn't. Is he?
>
> Mary: No, he's a special baby. Do you like babies?
>
> Dick: I got a baby sister at home. She's always raisin' heck.
>
> Eddie: She ain't a Jesus baby, that's why. That's the Jesus baby.
>
> Dick: Won't *he* be naughty?
>
> Mary (*smiling*): Probably, when he's little.
>
> Eddie: Just like us kids?
>
> Mary: Just like you kids.
>
> Gary: What will he be when he gets big?
>
> Dick: He'll be God, won't he?
>
> Mary: He's going to die, so all the kids like you can live.
>
> Joseph: You'll understand someday.
>
> Eddie: He's a nice baby.
>
> Mary: See? He's smiling. He likes you!
>
> All: We like him. Merry Christmas, little Lord Jesus.
>
> Mary: He says "Merry Christmas" too. To everyone in this room.

At a subsequent rehearsal, I brought out my guitar, a battered twelve-dollar campaigner that served as our only musical instrument. It was not very musical. We had sung along with it, though, with fair success. Songs like "I've Been Working on the Railroad" and "I Had a Little Chicken but She Wouldn't Lay an Egg" had been popular before Christmas. Now our attention was centered on two more seasonal numbers to be sung at the end of the program. One of them was "The Friendly Beasts," an old carol I remembered from when I was myself in the second grade. It was a sweet song, its story told through the mouths of the animals that gathered around the manger—the donkey and the cow and the ram and a pair of doves in the rafters. I knew the children would like the animal angle, and they sang the lyrics as mightily as their few and untrained voices would allow. The other carol was "Away in a Manger."

"I love Thee Lord Jesus, look down from the sky," we chorused, "and stay by my cradle till morning is nigh."

"All right for today," I announced. "First-graders can wash for lunch, and then the rest of you."

I repaired to the teacherage for my own standard fare of soup and sandwich. The rehearsals were coming along.

An enormous pine tree came to school Monday in the back of one of the ranch pickups. Unexpected volunteer labor at recess got it mounted in an old tire rim and maneuvered inside the schoolroom, where we wired it in stationary splendor in the library corner. Lights, supplied by a friendly teacher in town, were strung through its branches. And we decorated the bulletin board with her second gift, a wonderful array of Santa Claus and other Christmas pictures. The third and most wonderful of all lay hidden in my dresser drawer. It was a Santa Claus suit!

A cheap little phonograph had been bought in town to help out on the music front—In addition to playing records, it had a small microphone attachment. With this marvelous device we had much incentive for extra rehearsing, even after school. The children were thrilled to hear one another's voices coming over what sounded like the radio. And Gene was induced to broadcast his heretofore stumbling lines from Luke with unheard-of vigor and style.

"And the angel said to FEAR NOT," he thundered forth. "For LO, I bring you tidings of GREAT JOY which shall be unto you and all people." I was less astonished at his miraculous reading improvement than I would have been at any other time. For Christmas is a time of miracles, and here at the school we were making our own.

The tree blossomed forth with paper chains and pinecones and silver nuts willed to us by last year's art classes; it bore colored balls we made ourselves and glittering icicles twisted from strips of tin inside coffee cans, and stars of gold cut with tin snips from the insides of common cans. And the kittens, finding this a time of exceeding great joy, clambered to the topmost branches of the tree and found a hundred dangling delights to play with, while the puppy pulled every ornament off the lower branches and hid them all under the stove. Curiously, no one minded because Christmas was very strong upon the air. And rumors went forth that Santa Claus would come to the play, wearing his red suit this year.

The red suit lay shrouded in secrecy in my drawer, was also shrouded with a certain air of suspense; nobody had yet been found to wear it. I made a special horseback trip to the ranch looking for a volunteer. Discouraged by his lack of popularity, last year's Santa Claus—he of the bearskin coat—gave a flat no. And Doc said no sir, he wasn't going to wear a bunch of pillows and be Santa Claus; besides, he and Wayne and Fuzzy were all going to town to get drunk on the night of the play.

"We're going to town in a little red wagon, two wheels up and the other two a-draggin,'" he chanted happily—and returned to his duties with the pigs.

Who else was there? Billy's father, I thought, and set off at a lope for his house.

He gave me an incredulous stare. "Me?" he asked. "Santa Claus? He-ell, no!"

"What are we going to do, Annie?" I asked my gray mare as we back-tracked toward the school. Gene's father had refused. So had Leslie's and Pansy's. There was no use asking Dick's and Gary's. In a last-ditch attempt, I rode over to our neighbors, the Millers, and tied Annie to the fence outside.

"Couldn't you talk Bob into being Santa Claus for just half an hour?" I pleaded.

"I doubt it," laughed Mrs. Miller. "You know Bob. He's pretty leery of anything like that."

Bob was indeed leery when he heard about it. It began to look as if Santa Claus wouldn't make it after all.

We borrowed costumes from the as yet unmailed Old Clothes Drive, thanking the poster girl Caroline for her generosity in letting us use them one more time. Pansy as Mary was beautiful in an old blue silk dress worn backward for a straighter line, and topped by a graceful white shawl about her head. The shepherds were magnificent in bathrobes and raincoats, with flaming silk bandanas flowing from their heads in Christmas-card shepherd style.

We devoted a frantic last afternoon to making gifts, stapling paper together to make pads for various parent purposes, and crafting greeting cards of black art paper with tinselly green- and red- and rainbow-colored trees. Presents and cards piled up under the now magnificent tree.

As soon as the children had gone home I saddled Annie and galloped down the road to borrow a mop—and search once again for a Santa Claus. The neighbors were still adamant. Suspense terrific. And the time was at hand.

At 8:00 P.M., all actors were backstage and in costume. Three blankets were strung across the schoolroom to form the curtain; the audience was assembled in front, talking and smoking; an overture of carol music from the screechy phonograph sounded through the room, supervised by Gene. In back, the last makeup of colored chalk was carefully applied. Beneath the chalk, faces flushed in readiness. "Okay," I signaled Gene. "Ready. Set. Go."

The carol music faded. Up came the chorus of childish voices from behind the curtain, sounding though the darkened schoolroom:

> Why do bells for Christmas ring?
> Why do little children sing?
> Why do bells for Christmas ring?
> Why do little children sing?

The solo answers came back from Pansy and Bill, almost too soft to hear through the muffling curtains:

> Once a lovely shining star
> Seen by angels from afar . . .

Restless, the audience craned to see behind the curtain. A few caught the words, but the magic was softly spoken, subtly hard to hear:

And his mother sang, and smiled;
This is Christ, the Holy Child.
So the bells for Christmas ring,
So the little children sing.

Then the cheap loudspeaker rang out with Gene's thunderous rendition of Luke, after which Mary and Joseph were heard talking. The curtain lurched open to show them in front of the inn door. Mary, standing straight up, was about six inches shorter than Joseph on his knees. They knocked, and at last the innkeeper—Billy—appeared in black drapery and a yellow nightcap. He was intent and serious. No giggles.

"What do you want?" he demanded.

"We need lodging," croaked Joseph, "for the night."

"But I have none," said Billy. "There is a thousand strangers in town. All our space is taken."

"But we have come far today, and Mary is ill." Mary wavered in a sickly fashion, not hamming it, just right.

"I tell you we have no room!" began Billy—and forgot the next line. "... Uh ..."

"People!" I whispered loudly from backstage.

"... People are sleeping on the floor. There isn't an inch left."

Looking heartbroken, Mary and Joseph began to turn away into the cold night. The innkeeper's face struggled a moment.

"Halloo!" he cried. "Stop a minute! I have a stable that can shelter you from the wind."

Back turned Mary and Joseph, going with him through the door of the inn, into the darkness that was supposed to lead to the warm stable and safety. In fact it led to the teacherage. There had been no way to stage the stable, with our limited space and equipment, and the limited memories of our children. They couldn't do more than two full scenes in front of the curtain; behind it, I could coach them easily. So our stable and its animals had to depend on the limited imaginations of the audience, plus the teacherage.

They had to imagine Mary and Joseph lying down in the straw of an empty stall, accompanied by the sounds of animals moving and rustling in the warm dark. "It's warm here," spoke Mary's voice, "and the animals seem so friendly."

"Our donkey is glad of a rest too," said Joseph. "Faithful donkey—he carried you so far! Listen! Is he saying something or am I dreaming?"

Now, the voices rose in the old, old carol:

> I, said the donkey, all shaggy and brown,
> I carried his mother uphill and down,
> I carried his mother to Bethlehem town,
> I, said the donkey, shaggy and brown.

"And the cow and the ram!" exclaimed Mary, "Joseph, do you hear them?"

> I, said the cow, all white and red,
> I gave him my manger for a bed,
> I gave him my hay to pillow his head.
> I, said the cow, all white and red.

> I, said the ram, with the curling horn,
> I gave him my wool that he might be warm,
> He wore my coat on Christmas morn,
> I, said the ram, with curling horn.

Now they were all singing!

> Jesus our brother kind and good,
> In Bethlehem born in stable rude,
> The friendly beasts around him stood,
> Jesus our brother, kind and good.

The voices and guitar trailed off into a hushed silence. There was a bit of bumping backstage, and in a moment the curtain opened to show Mary and Joseph leaning over the baby, in the brightness of Christmas morning. The baby—Pansy's doll—was swaddled in dishtowels and reclining in a manger made of an old sawhorse bedded with Annie's hay. At the appointed moment, the shepherds knocked loudly and bustled onstage.

"We came as fast as we could," announced Leslie, "to wash up the child."

"We are glad to see you," said Mary.

"We have no gifts," explained Billy, "only ourselves."

"He needs no gifts," Mary said. "Are you shepherds?"

"Our sheep," said Leslie with a royal sweep of the hand, "is lyin' out in the snow."

"Last night we heard singing . . ."

"And saw the star . . ."

"And then the angels came . . ."

There was a knock at the door of the teacherage behind them. Somehow the children kept going as I hurried to open it. The angels had indeed come! There, swaying back and forth in the cold, stood Wayne and Fuzzy and Doc. The smell of town was potent in their clouds of frosty breath.

"I guessh we got here okay," said Doc. "We're in time ain't we?"

He plumped down an armload of packages on the back step. "Where's that Santa Claus suit?"

"Just a minute," I said joyfully. "I'll get it! Oh, Doc, you are wonderful!"

On stage, the children were proceeding. "Will he be naughty?" Dick was asking.

"Probably, when he's little," Mary replied.

"Just like you kids."

I hustled the Santa Claus suit out to Doc, who tucked it under his coat. "The presents can go in that green gunny sack on the front porch," I told him. "Wayne, you watch the door and don't let any of the kids see him. Here, tie this scarf around your face and head somehow. We'll be ready for you in just a moment. Hurry!"

Santa Claus and his cohort vanished rather unsteadily into the darkness. I picked up the old guitar and hurried to join the children as "Away in a Manger" rose thinly but mightily into the air. They were singing more strongly than ever, sweeter, with a look on their faces that gave me a shivery feeling. Were these my children? Or was the little girl whose face shone with such a transcendent glow momentarily someone else? Were the boys my boys? Or had they seen and caught some whiff of two thousand years ago? No, of course not—and yet there was that look about their faces, for an electric instant or two, as they turned toward the baby.

I love Thee Lord Jesus, look down from the sky,
And stay by my cradle till morning is nigh.

The spell snapped as the curtain closed. The children crowded around me to get faces cleaned and costumes unpinned, while Gene plugged in the phonograph and the choir music began again. I poked my head out in front a little nervously, wondering if Santa Claus had navigated around to the front door all right. A reassuring stumping and stamping sounded from that direction, and little brothers and sisters were already aflame with excitement touched off by glimpses of red through the porch window.

The last red smudge came off Dick's grimacing cheek, and I quickly slipped around to the front porch to see if all was in order. Santa Claus, reinforced by another three or four slugs of Christmas cheer, was ready—and all eyes awaited him. With a wonderful series of Ho Ho Ho's, amid a rising crescendo from the children, he dramatically stomped into the room.

I walked slowly to the back door, enjoying the sharp cold a moment before going in again. The air was marvelously clear. And over in the east, wasn't there an *awfully* bright star?

CHAPTER SEVEN

Schoolhouse in the Spring

As April stole with moccasined feet over the gumbo hills, we all turned Indian. Maybe it was the whisper of ancient times in the warm wind that made us think about people who had hunted and fought across the greening land so long before we arrived. Maybe it was the innate primitive in all small children. Whatever our reasons, we found a worthy purpose for our doings in the Montana course of study, which prescribed a unit for third-grade social studies called "How the Indians Lived."

Billy was the sole third-grader, but the others could enjoy and appreciate the work as well as he.

We began our discussion on the day the county superintendent, with her driver, chose to visit us on her routine annual visit. A bright-eyed gathering of all but Gene, who was working on geography at his seat, were perched on the cottonwood stumps in the first-grade corner. Our visitors sat off to one side as the children began to contribute facts concerning Montana's first citizens.

Enthusiasm ran high as the children described what Indians and cowboys did to each other in the movies—until it seemed we were getting off track. I suggested making a list of the actual facts we already knew. The list developed as follows: (1) Indians rode bareback, (2) Indians hunted buffalo, (3) Indians fought against white men, (4) Indians wore few clothes—and some, in Leslie's words, even went barenaked, (5) Indians shot bows and arrows, (6) Indians scalped people, and (7) some Indians had tails—an item offered by Gary, who insisted he had seen a picture of a tailed Indian in a book.

This "fact" demanded looking into at once. Gary was requested to produce his evidence. With pompous assurance, he marched over to the bookcase and pulled out my battered copy of *War Paint: An Indian Pony*, by Paul Brown. Breathlessly we waited while he leafed through the pages, at last pausing at a vivid picture. It showed a mounted Indian, very nearly bare-naked, galloping pell-mell away from the enemy. And sure enough, as Gary pointed out in triumph, there was *his tail*—a long breechclout, which flew out from his buttocks in a very tail-like manner. The class was enchanted, and Gary nearly burst with pride. It took some time for me to explain to the children about breechclouts and to persuade them that Indians, like other people, were positively, absolutely, tail-less.

Once begun, the unit led to some fascinating explorations. A coloring book about Indians from the dime store in town proved the perfect teaching device as the children studied and carefully colored each large picture.

Four main geographical culture areas were soon learned, along with some of the tribes that had peopled them: roach-headed canoeists in the Eastern Woodlands; shepherds and silversmiths in the Southwest, who lived in pueblos and hogans on the hot desert; our own tipi-dwelling horsemen of the plains; and the bold fishermen of the Northwest, carvers of tall totem poles. The children became adept at finding wrong details in the coloring book pictures. A coastal Indian would simply not be wearing a feather war bonnet; and a tipi scene of camp life on the plains was dead wrong if it contained a totem pole or canoe or a turquoise necklace.

At last the coloring was completed, following painstaking attention to correctness, such as the matter of how to properly color a fringed suit. It would be made of buckskin, they knew, and therefore should be white or tan—no blues or purples, please!—except on the border of porcupine-quill trimming. Carefully, we picked out the best and most authentic pictures to illustrate our four selected areas, and pasted these on large wall charts, labeling each appropriately and adding a descriptive story about the particular place. After pinning them up in a border above the blackboards, we were quite proud of them and were beginning to feel like real experts.

Before long the children expressed much interest in the Indians of today, asking many questions about those who still lived in Montana. It seemed a wonderful chance to explore the problems of a minority group, and I began to dream of a field trip to visit a government school at Birney on the Northern Cheyenne reservation sixty miles away, where I was later to teach for four years. The teacher there—a personal acquaintance of mine—would have received us most kindly. A day spent among real Indian children would teach more at first hand than three weeks of studying pictures and books. But the parents felt that it was too far to travel and too impractical to be considered at all. The blow fell hard, especially since the children and parents at the neighboring Garland School, hearing of the idea, were happily planning to join us and go!

We smothered our disappointment by preparing a lively program for Mother's Day. Related only vaguely to what we had been studying, it turned out to be a merry affair. We planned in advance to gather needed props and supplies. Drums and feathers would be necessary; also a campfire of sorts, and a stage setting that would somehow suggest a tipi. In a climactic war dance scene, rattles and moccasins would also come in handy. With whoops and hollers, the kids went home to look for these items.

Next morning there hove into sight a large and foreign brand of bird. It was ostrich-sized or bigger, with tufts of feathers jutting out on all sides, and behind it lumbered an identical mate. Together they approached the school, and only when two feather-muffled voices issued forth with "Good morning, Miss Margot" did I recognize Gary and Dick.

Ignorant of the number of feathers produced per turkey, my first thought was that they must have stripped every gobbler in the country. But within two hours the previous afternoon, they had found their feathery prizes around the Millers' bushes, where the birds had shed enough feathers to fill five or six cans.

Later that afternoon, using strips of gunny sacks for headbands, the SH children made headdresses by poking turkey feathers all around the top of the wearer's head. The effect was remarkable—and it was not till weeks later that I remembered with horror that sometimes poultry possess lice. But none of our number ever complained.

The drums were less successful than the war bonnets. A small book on Indian handicrafts suggested cutting and stretching old inner tubes across big tin cans, an idea that had filled us with high hopes. The bigger the can, the louder the boom, according to the handicraft book. Gene was allowed to build the first drum in reward for a promptly finished arithmetic lesson. His struggles and grunts halfway through the process, however, called a halt to other work until we had all tried our best at helping him. The rubber was determined to fly off the top of the can, no matter how tightly it was lashed into place, and when pierced for lacing through from top to bottom, it promptly tore. Gene finally achieved one little drum, built on the frame of a two-pound coffee can. But it was rather a dud, and nobody dared hit it very hard. In the program later on, the drum section was very weak. The tin can section, on the other hand, did nobly.

Part of the tin can section performed so nobly in rehearsal, in fact, that it had to be outlawed. The instructions for making the instruments came from the same handicrafts book: Take a baking powder can and throw in a handful of small stones; put the top back on, and impale the apparatus on a long stick. You now have an instrument we shall call a "tin can jangle rattle."

Our own tin can jangle rattle was such a deafening success that the teacher could not hear herself think, much to the delight of Eddie and Gary, who took turns jangling the instrument as they paraded crashingly around the schoolyard and were probably heard at the main ranch. The thing was appallingly loud. I made them restrict its use to recess, thinking that whatever tribe invented such a gadget must have had powerful ghosts to drive away, maybe even DT's.

The Mother's Day play revolved around a hard-working Indian lady, Pretty Beaver, and her worthless husband, Big Lazy Buck. Adapted from an old folk tale, it told the story of their exchanging places for a day, the woman emerging triumphant from her success in doing manly work but the man ending up a total wreck after his bout with domesticity. Billy was Big Lazy Buck, who was too lazy to go hunting. Pretty Beaver, played by Pansy, went one day to teach him a lesson— leaving her husband home at the mercy of their "Hollering Papoose," portrayed by Dick.

The whole thing was poorly prepared and rehearsed, but we laughed ourselves silly over it. For the night of the program, we made tin-can lanterns by punching patterns of nail holes in empty tin cans and setting within each a lighted candle. A number of them placed about the schoolroom gave off a soft twinkling shimmer almost starlike in quality, as the flames flickered inside the rows of little holes. In such a setting, Gene walked out to greet the assembled parents, reading less painfully than at Christmastime the following message:

> This started out to be a play for Mother's Day. Everybody knows that mother works harder than anyone else in the family, but the only trouble is most of the men won't admit it. So we decided to put on a play that would show how hard the women work. Even the women in an Indian camp did most of the hard work, so here is a story about one who got tired of her lazy husband.
>
> Lazy Buck would not hunt buffalo, so his wife and papoose got hungry. Pretty Beaver decided she would go hunting and show him how to do it. When Lazy Buck stayed home, he had a terrible time and everything went wrong. By the time his wife got back he was a changed Indian because she really taught him a lesson.
>
> This is a funny way to say that we all like our mothers pretty well, even if nobody talks about it very much.

Such a sentiment won a round of applause from the visiting matrons, who had just borne their usual contributions of cake and coffee into the teacherage, and were in a mood to be appreciated. As the play progressed, nobody was too sure of the plot, but Hollering Papoose bawled so lustily and beat his heels on the floor in such uproarious tantrums that the audience howled with pleasure. At the closing scene, when the warriors and Pretty Beaver returned loaded with meat, the dance created sheer havoc. Bonnets flopping, the younger six pranced and lurched around the crepe-paper fire, chanting "Honny wa yah he naya" at the top of their lungs while Gene, as Big Heap Chief, pounded solemnly on the drum. Most of the feathers had shaken loose and scattered across the floor by the time our weary warriors hopped into the teacherage and ended the show. It was the most popular of our school programs.

The Indian mood stayed with us until the end of school. With bows and arrows they had built at home, the children had many a session of target practice at recess, and the schoolyard rang with shrill war cries on many a sunny spring morning.

Outdoor recess had been a real problem all year because the children were so few and so widespread in age. There were never enough children for two teams, and the teams that went ahead and played anyhow were never remotely equal. Whatever they did play, the same people won and lost. It is one thing to find games for an even group of twenty or thirty players, and quite another to do so for four tiny boys, two middle-sizers, and an athletic giant in the seventh grade, plus a girl. It was natural for the children to idolize Gene, and he bossed over every activity from bouncing on the seesaw to games of tag or stealing sticks. Billy followed at his heels, exerting his authority occasionally from the second-in-command status of the third grade. The rest tagged along happily when they were on Gene's side and unhappily when they were not; in fact, contentment during school hours depended on whether or not you'd been on Gene's team in the last recess game.

The obvious course of action was to capitalize on Gene's leadership and get him to teach the others new games—as a sort of coach. But when it came to recess, he wasn't the least interested in cooperating with a teacher, preferring to boss the children in his own way. His apathetic response floored me. And nothing changed until the rope situation finally reached a crisis.

The ropes had come to school on the second day, and I had welcomed them, thinking that they could be used in lieu of swings if we attached them to the bare log frame the men had erected for us. Or possibly they could work as jump ropes. Neither suggestion was taken up, despite the liveliest rope-jumping demonstration I could manage. Indeed not! Other uses were found for them, which luckily did not kill anyone.

The first use involved mountain climbing, or as close an imitation as possible. Inspired by my friends' exhibition on the schoolhouse, the children tried a few daredevil ascensions of their own, the ropes wound about their middles as Nate's had been. It was not unusual to find at recess one or two daring figures perched mountaineer-style upon one of the toilets or the woodshed. If they slipped they were likely to dangle perilously until rescued by Gene. Fearing that someone would lynch himself, I made them stop. But Dick and Billy had almost called a halt to the procedure by themselves. Dick, afraid of the attempt himself, had been watching Billy struggle to the top of the boys' toilet and then get to his feet triumphantly on the sloping roof. At that precise moment, the roof began to creak dangerously.

"Get down Billy, get down quick," Dick had screamed, "or you are going to fall down that toilet hole!"

Billy's descent had more speed than dignity, and he was teased for weeks about what might have happened to him if he'd really fallen through into the yawning privy pit.

No longer in the mountain-climbing mood, the children turned their attention to the game of Wild Stallion. Somebody wielded a rope, and somebody else was the wild stallion, who dodged about with panicky whinnies until roped around the heels by his pursuer and thrown end over end on the ground. He was then hogtied, branded, and earmarked—the latter sometimes painfully—and finally turned loose. Billy and Gene were of course the most successful ropers, and after a hard fall or two the rest did not enjoy the game as much as they had at first. But still, they all insisted they wanted to play.

Something had to be done, but I wasn't sure just what. The children had been kept in for playing too rough, scolded, reasoned with, and consulted for suggestions to improve our playground sport. None said anything; and Gene, who was responsible, infuriated me by staring at his fingertips and shrugging his shoulders as if to say "I don't care, you're not going to bother me."

The situation drifted along unresolved until one day of total, glorious Montana mud. I stayed in at recess to prepare some paints for artwork, and glanced outside after a few minutes to view a scene of horror. Gene was dragging Gary by a rope feetfirst through the mud, followed worshipfully by all the rest of them, whose clothes showed plainly they had had their turn. That was the end, both of my patience and of the game of Wild Stallion, forevermore.

"STOP THAT RIGHT THIS MINUTE!" I roared, in a bellow that rattled the top of the windmill. A gumbo-plastered figure arose weakly to his feet, and they all stood there rather foolishly. "I AM ASHAMED OF EVERY ONE OF YOU, and if you CAN'T DO ANYTHING WITH THOSE ROPES EXCEPT DRAG LITTLE KIDS AROUND IN THE MUD then we will have NO MORE ROPES IN THIS SCHOOL EVER AGAIN."

In stunned silence, they trudged squishily back into the school. The teacher had never yelled like that before! Every overshoe was placed in its own cubbyhole with scrupulous care. "Mercy," I thought—surprised at myself. "It works like a charm!" And the ropes went home with their owners that night for good.

Next day we all repaired outside and sat on the steps in the sun, ready to decide on a course of action. I delivered a less passionate lecture about why we didn't roll people around in the mud if we could help it, and I asked for help. What could we do for fun out here, with such a mixture of kids?

For a few minutes, the silence was profound. Pansy was a girl and therefore, by majority consensus, didn't count. The four little boys had nothing to say because they had never been in school before and had no idea what organized play was. Billy and Gene picked at their finger-nails in silence. Billy had gone to town school the year before but didn't see how any of the town games could work here, and Gene had never been in school with more than six other children, for whom he was always the oldest and undisputed boss.

Finally Gene offered the thought that some new playground equipment would help matters, so the school supply catalog was fetched and its pages scanned with care. They knew that we didn't have much money, and a budget was set at twenty dollars or less.

It was a real mental exercise to find things for less than twenty dollars. All the good, tough balls cost ten dollars or more, and we wanted a bat too, and some blocks, and a basketball goal, which was promoted by Gene, so of course all the rest wanted it. The catalog also displayed pages of footballs, and tumbling mats, and beautiful slides and swings, all of which were far beyond our means. "Aw, phoo hecky on all that fancy stuff," commented Leslie philosophically. "We don't need nothing like that."

Our purchase order finally included:
1 cheap rubber playground ball, listed as all-purpose
1 baseball bat
1 basketball ring and net
1 set of blocks
1 set of ring toss

In addition, the children decided that I was to look for ideas on games to play under our peculiar conditions. And finally, to our surprise, Billy offered to teach the game of Pom Pom Pull Away he had learned in town. For the meantime, the crisis was over. We went inside, where Gene was set to work filling out the order form. It took him all afternoon.

Delving into the matter of playground games brought forth one other suggestion that at least seemed worth trying. It was called Tether Ball. A small ball was attached to the top of a pole by a length of rope. Two players stood on opposite sides, hitting at the ball with wooden paddles until one or the other of them succeeded in winding it up snugly around the pole. It would not be hard to build, once we had set up a pole, so we decided to go ahead with it.

A survey of the school grounds disclosed a pole, which was crooked, but long and stout. Gene was sent off at noon to get a posthole digger—a mission that brought him glory since it entailed the privilege of driving my car, temporarily, on this side of the river. With grunting and groaning, the younger children managed to saw through both splintered ends of the heavy log, readying one end to be set in the ground and the other to hold the nail that would hold the rope. We all cheered when the ends fell off; for such little ones it was a hard job, and they had stuck to it with grim determination. Nonchalantly, with the air of a bygone expert at such work, Gene dug the hole, though not very fast. When it was deep enough, we dragged the pole over to it and lined up beside its full length as it lay on the ground. Each child had a particular spot to grab hold of and hoist for all he was worth, with Gene on the far end, where his long arms could boost it highest in the air. With a mighty heave ho, up she went!—much in the manner of the marines hoisting the flagpole on Iwo Jima. It stood upright—a monument to our efforts. Somewhat crooked and wiggly, it worked fine after I knotted our little hardball into the pants leg of a pair of children's long underwear that came out of the rag bag and attached it to the top of the pole with three tied-together scraps of clothesline. With boards to use as paddles, the children shrieked with glee all the remaining recesses and stayed voluntarily after school to play some more.

Billy's game of Pom Pom Pull Away became so popular it was played almost to death, until Gene taught the kids to play stealing sticks as well. After that, recesses were fairly well busied with those two activities. Our resources were supplemented with a small card file of game suggestions that could be resorted to in emergencies. In March the men finally put up the swings. My gray mare Annie nearly leapt over the fence for good the first time she saw Dick and Gary hurtling birdlike back and forth through the air.

It was not until late spring that we had another playground crisis. It took some time in building up—and it was a pretty good one. The SH children, like all children, had to learn how to take care of things, but how to teach such responsibility is not always obvious to the novice teacher. Harping at children not to do this or that is sometimes less effective than letting the worst happen one time; after that they may know what you are talking about. With this in mind, I had watched the swing chains on our none-too-sturdy equipment being worn thinner and thinner, and decided to wait until the first one broke before saying anything. They were being plenty rough on them, and milder warnings had done little good.

Disaster had been imminent for two weeks when the calamity finally befell a temporarily guileless Billy. As predicted, one of the chains had snapped, dumping him unhurt but astonished on the dusty ground. The time had come to talk things over.

"Look," I said, "it's about time we decided what to do about this playground stuff. We haven't taken care of it well enough, and now it's starting to fall apart."

Heads nodded as I continued. They had not been scolded ahead of time, I explained, because it would be better if they saw for themselves what could happen. Did they remember the trapeze acts they had invented so artistically, with the whole school suspended from two swings in a flying wedge formation?

"Them swings was only made for one person. Ted said so," recalled Eddie thoughtfully.

"Yeah, and you guys swung too high, too," said Leslie. "Papa said don't go way up 'cause the chains would break. And Billy he was up so high he could see clear over the chimney."

"Shouldn't have swung double," announced Dick. "*I* knew we wasn't supposed to."

"Well you did it anyway," commented Pansy.

Eddie's face was puckered with concentration. "Well Billy was all by himself when the swing broke," he said finally. "Wasn't anybody on there double when she broke." To Eddie that was pretty good indication that swinging double hadn't done it; it had just broken all by itself.

"Do you think you fellows put too much of a load on it and wore it out a long time ago?" I asked.

"Well I don't care," announced Gary with a lower lip that poked out two inches from his deceptively angelic face. Gary was in a pronounced "I don't care" stage.

We all ignored him and continued the discussion, recollecting other cases of misused equipment, like the bucking horse games on the seesaw, where Gene on one end was pitted against the entire rest of the school on the other until, jerking wildly to and fro, most of the riders fell off on their noggins.

"Can you see that things really do break if you use them too hard?" I asked.

"*Yes*," said Pansy with righteous indignation. She hated the boys' roughness.

"What would you like to do about this? It's up to you."

"Make it a goop," offered Eddie. ("Goops" were penalties awarded to people who did bad things.) The rest concurred, and we went back to work with a clear understanding. Only one person at a time on the swings and only two people on the teeter-totter.

But now, a week later, the second swing dangled uselessly from its broken chain. Leslie and Gene had violated the rule and had been on it together. Ignorance of the law was no excuse because we all knew that everybody had helped make the law.

The two culprits were called in from the playground. Carefully they avoided each other's gaze—and mine.

"All right," I snapped wrathfully. "Just exactly what happened?"

Gene, it appeared, had been sitting rather inactively in the swing when Leslie jumped up on top of him. Gene maintained that he had told Leslie to get off, which was doubtful, but Leslie had nothing to say in his own defense. And the upshot of it all was obvious when the chain cracked, and down they both came.

Out the window, the other children huddled in a conclave around the broken swing, discussing what had happened. They were called in so we could get all stories straight, which took on the atmosphere of a grand jury trial. The five innocent judge-witnesses brought forth the facts. Leslie was definitely to blame. He had even done it once before, and when reminded by the others about the rule, he obviously didn't care. He had even jeered at them in a most unrepentant fashion.

Moreover, they said, in this case Gene had told Leslie to get down. Five small heads nodded solemnly.

Encouraged by testimony from the crowd, Gene rose to his own defense. "I could have knocked Leslie down or been real rough, but I didn't want to do *that*," he said piously, his nobility settling round him like a royal cape. No longer was he accused in so undignified a fashion! The trial went on.

"Did Leslie know he wasn't supposed to do that?" I asked.

The answer was unanimously "yes."

"Should we punish him or let him go?" was the next question.

"PUNISH HIM," chorused six voices. Leslie was sitting stiff and straight as a Spartan, looking straight ahead, betraying no emotion whatever. (I had intended to punish Leslie anyway but was glad the indictment came from his peers. More effective that way.)

"Why do you think grown people punish kids?

"Make 'em mind," said Billy sourly.

"Doesn't do any good, though," commented Gene. "Just makes the kids madder."

"You gotta do something to 'em," said Dick.

"That's the only way the kids learn some things, I guess," said Pansy sadly. "When their tail ends is hurting."

"Let's give Leslie a whipping!" shouted Gary, with joyous anticipation.

"Would that make him really remember?" I asked, not wanting to tackle Leslie physically.

They finally decided it wouldn't do much good.

"How about keeping him after school?" suggested Billy.

"Or sending a note home to his mother?" I put in.

"Yes, but you got to send it to Ted too, not just Ruthie," Eddie said firmly. The others agreed enthusiastically, and so the sentence was decided. Sending a note home! That had never happened to anybody all year.

A pencil and paper were brought out, while fourteen doom-sensing eyes followed my every movement. "You have to write it," I said to the group. "Tell me what to say."

Leslie had not moved in his seat but looked straight ahead of him. I stifled a pang of pity as we all set about composing the note, which read as follows when it went home in Leslie's lunch pail that evening:

Dear Ruthie and Ted,

All the schoolchildren including Leslie are writing this note to you. Leslie broke one swing today. Gene was in the swing and Leslie jumped up on it. We made a rule before that only one person could swing at once, and only two people teeter-totter. Gene told him to get off and finally both of them went down. That was our last swing and now it is gone.

Signed: Gary
Eddie
Dick
Leslie
Bill
Pansy
Gene

This epistle was given its due regard at Leslie's home that evening, but the lesson had already gone home sufficiently.

We had a chance to demonstrate our athletic skills in a more constructive way on a fine day in May, at the track meet and spelling bee held for all the rural schools by the Kiwanis Club in Miles City. It was an exciting outing for all of us, as two hundred or more country children would be pouring into town with their parents and teachers for a taste of city life. I drove in with the Jones boys, after the sternest warnings that they must sit still and act like gentlemen, which they did flawlessly.

The other children traveled with their families, planning to meet us at the first scheduled stop—the spelling bee.

The spelling bee had classes for only the third grade on up, and fortunately we were late for it. Gene—with some previous distasteful experience at spelling bees—didn't want to spell in any case. And our reputation as a school might have suffered with Billy its only speller, though he might have refused at the last minute to participate anyway.

As it was, we stood and watched the others. Groups of nervous children, each headed by a harassed town businessman, were doing their best to spell forth against the general din in a huge upstairs hall.

"Attempt," he would pronounce. "Attempt."

"What?" the speller would ask, craning his neck.

"Attempt, ATTEMPT!" the businessman repeated, slightly irked after three or four such repetitions. At length the child attempted to spell the word, and the turn passed to someone else, while in the next group another businessman was encountering the same situation.

On gazing about the hall, lined five-rows-deep with spectators, one had several pertinent reflections. There were a lot of rural school children when you saw them *en masse!* And there was quite a variety— from the laughing, sophisticated eighth-grade girls, rouged and curled for the occasion, to the bewildered little boy clinging to Miss Miller's hand with a look of vacancy in his eyes. And as I watched, the door opened to admit another rural pupil—the twenty-year-old blind girl, whose reading in Braille had required so many hours of work from her patient teacher. What a job these schools had! And how limited were their resources in dealing with special children, except for the teachers themselves, who often gave so heroically.

The first-graders in my group began to get restless, so we all departed shortly for the airport, where three jet airplanes from the army performed for our special benefit, rushing past over our heads several times—so close we could almost touch them. One even landed on the field, permitting the children to swarm all over it.

After that we ate a free dinner at the fairgrounds, and adjourned to the races. The children all entered, and Dick and Gene won ribbons. Gene got teased and discussed by the town girls, and Dick's ribbon was a real triumph.

We returned home to tragedy, however, for Longtail the Mouse was dead. Pansy buried him, with flowers.

➹

During the spring, the playground acquired one more asset, which the children built themselves. It was meant to be a clubhouse because in February we had organized a club. Intended for promoting good times and civic improvements, the club had met once a week after school, with dues of a penny a week and refreshments ranging from lollipops to a sack of pastel-colored marshmallows. During our first meetings, we spent most of the time attempting rather futilely to dig an outdoor fire pit in the still frozen ground.

Later, when the days grew warmer, construction of the clubhouse began. The children used the back wall of the coal shed as one support, employing most of the junk lumber that had formerly been stacked there. The first-graders measured and sawed like mad, biting their tongues in concentration. We had no posthole digger this time, so the required holes were dug by hand. Pansy and Billy led the way by pushing tin cans in the still-hard ground.

Gene, in another of his disinterested spells, declined to have anything to do with the clubhouse project and was constantly wooing the younger children away from it to follow him in some other sport. By now I knew better than to force them to finish it or even to promote the idea too hard. What did I care whether or not they finished the silly clubhouse?

The ruse worked. Two days after they had abandoned their tools, Billy rushed up breathlessly at recess time.

"Miss Margot," he said importantly, "we want to finish up that clubhouse out there, Dick and me."

"All right," I told him. "Go ahead."

And go ahead they did—Billy and Dick by themselves, with the greatest enthusiasm. Billy, my recalcitrant problem child, the discipline case of months before! And Dick, who of all the children, hero-worshipped and followed Gene the most faithfully! The others played around for a while, but as if against their will they were drawn over to watch the carpenters. Before long Pansy was helping them, then Eddie, and at long last Gary and Leslie.

Gene, his following dissolved, pretended to pay no attention to them, but at last he too weakened. If they were determined to build the clubhouse, he had better take hold and show them how! Seizing the best hammer, he began giving orders as if he had thought of the whole thing himself. And they worked furiously for a half hour after recess was supposed to be over, while the teacher was inside congratulating herself.

The club also led to a flurry of interest in money and banking. Our penny-a-week dues had to be kept track of, and the whole matter complicated itself when some children began bringing nickels and dimes to pay ahead. The knotty problems that arose were somewhat elementary for Gene but real brain teasers for Pansy and Billy, who were given the job of running the school bank. A record was kept of all the money deposited in a large glass jar, and of who deposited it, since the money was divided into seven accounts for the seven children. When a child wanted to withdraw from his account, he wrote a check—out of an old checkbook or simply on a slip of paper stating the amount and his name. The club dues, aggregating at seven cents a week, had to be kept separate from the other deposits. And the total capital assets of the bank skyrocketed when Leslie appeared one morning with six dimes, which he had robbed, we later learned, from the piggy bank at home belonging jointly to his sisters and brothers!

Pansy and Billy struggled and pondered over the seven accounts. Billy, after bouncing one check himself—he only had one cent in and paid two cents worth of dues—borrowed five cents from his little brother, which soon had to be transferred to his own account. Each week, seven cents for dues were subtracted from the seven deposits and moved into the club treasury, where all was counted and added up carefully to ensure that the records jibed with the cash on hand. Then, brows furrowed, the two financiers returned to the bank itself, where they laboriously counted the balance and added up the figures on the blackboard.

Sometimes it took them all recess to do the job satisfactorily, but they were determined to do it properly. And I don't think any two second- or third-graders could have known more about the complexities of money than did Pansy and Billy by the end of the year.

CHAPTER EIGHT

The Garland School and
the Other Side of the River

The Garland School stood firmly beside the road to town, its log walls a solid brown, its recently added teacherage spanking white, its stars and stripes fluttering proudly in the sun. It was our nearest institutional neighbor. Our only other was the pert, red-roofed Star Creek School, attended by "Aunt Betty's kids," where, lacking electricity, they held their dances in the dark. Star Creek was on our own side of the river, but it was twenty miles away, over awful roads. That left the Garland School as the closest and most tempting to visit, since one passed it on the way to town. Eight miles from our ranch gate, it was announced by yellow "SCHOOL" signs, a surprisingly bold marker on a road that failed to signal even its most violent, gravel-skittering curves. In fact the Garland School appeared to be quite pleased with itself; although a mere dot on the map, which it did possess, it was as well cared for and important as any single, staunch little building could be.

The dot on the map had in fact been earned in olden times before the school was built, when Garland had been a stopover station for stagecoaches on the two-day trip from Miles City to Sheridan. A weary driver could sleep there in a small shack, going on with fresh horses the next day. That shack, once abandoned, became the first Garland School.

"There was more kids in school that year than there's ever been since," a longtime rancher informed me. "It was better than fifty years ago, but I went there—along with nine others. We'd all crowd in there, and the roof was so low the schoolmom was always catching those splintery boards in her hair."

"Did you learn anything?" I asked.

"Yes ma'am I learned something! She was the best schoolmom I ever went to, young and blue-eyed and pretty. I was about half wild but she could sure handle me. Used to be stricter than hell in school time, really meaning business. And then she'd always keep me after school, and when the others went home she'd pull a sack of Durham out of her garter and we'd both roll a smoke. I was just twelve years old."

The stage shack, cramped and inconvenient, was the only available school at the turn of the century, when the state lacked either funds or the inclination to put up schoolhouses for such outlying districts as Garland. Finally, the citizens got mad—and decided to build their own. Logs, bought cheap off a neighboring ranch, were cut and hauled and erected by the local ranchers themselves. Bit by bit the building grew, until a roof finally covered it—and the neighborhood, despite all economies, found itself badly in debt.

What to do? There was, in the community, a piano, played skillfully by one of the local matrons, whose husband was equally adept on the violin. And the Garland dances in the new schoolhouse, based on these talents, commenced, with proceeds going toward paying the schoolhouse debt, which was eliminated after a few years of regular midnight revels, contests over the hand of the reigning teacher, much red liquor imbibed the way of all good liquor, and many a wavering journey home by the light of dawn via team or model A. Perhaps typical was the experience of Mr. Shy, who, journeying home, mistook each county mailbox for a sheep wagon driven by the sheriff, in hot pursuit, who would surely haul him off to town for the past evening's assorted misdeeds.

The schoolhouse, after fifty years, was new no longer, but it carried on in much of its old tradition. The dances, the way of life, the people themselves—little here had changed other than the growing up of a generation, the switch to trucks and cars, the gathering of more hay to sustain cattle throughout the winter. The changes might have seemed great to the people themselves. But time here had dealt a kinder hand to the old ways than in most places; the cards were less stacked in favor of wiping out the past, and there was no rushing into the future at breakneck speed. Television, telephones—many of these gods of the moment were missing. And it was not too painful to have it so.

In the Garland teacherage lived the merry Miss Miller, who turned out to be a lively friend. Margaret Miller was not so untutored a tutor as I, having attended teachers college and having already taught for two years. Her wisdom in the teaching trade reached marvelous depths, which I soon learned to reach to in times of need.

Margaret did her part as well in hosting the community dances at Garland. The floor shook, the rafters rattled, and Mrs. Bichle whisked by in a nimble schottische with old Mr. Jones, while coffee and boiled beef began to reach the consumption point in Margaret's teacherage. A baby, amid piles of overcoats, was sleeping in her bed. Margaret herself, in the schoolroom, was dancing with Ike Shy, the tall young man already rumored to be her forthcoming bridegroom. That tall young man, a nephew of the older Mr. Shy, was behaving decorously, but his brother, in the corner, was attempting to stand on his head. Outside, wagers were being made with Wayne—who had driven to the dance— that he could not, no, he would never *dare* to swallow an entire half-bottle of whiskey without stopping.

"Oh-ho-ho-HO," cried Wayne unsteadily. "You want to bet?"

A dollar was placed on the issue, and Wayne won it, putting himself out of the picture for the rest of the evening.

Indoors, the headstander tumbled over and skinned his cheekbone on a bench, while his mother forbiddingly scowled at him across the room, her reaction noticed by everyone except her performing offspring.

A little boy, grinning toothlessly, kept cutting in on the pairs of dancers and insisting on dancing too, three-hands-round. Miss Miller, whose feet were starting to hurt, was given not a moment's rest—but whirled from partner to partner in an endless round of cutting-in. Indeed, it would appear that a teacher yearning for a social life might try this apparently lonesome school. Nowhere else could she possibly be such a queen of local attention, such a belle of the local ball.

Supper was served, after an appropriate supper waltz. Plates were heaped high; coffee mugs smoldered. Mr. Shy, lurching as he settled himself on the floor, spilled a sprinkling of red baked beans.

"Haw, haw, Unk!" cried the headstander, now right-side up. "You got beans in your boots this time for sure, and I bet it'll take you ten years to get back up again."

"Hell!" snorted Mr. Shy. "I can get up faster than you can, sassy pup. Want to try?"

The headstander declined a contest. "Beans in your boots!" he repeated gleefully. "Christ, them poor beans."

Someone remarked that Mr. Shy was just packing his lunch for the next day.

"That's it okay!" crowed the headstander. "That's his lunch all right. Beans and toe cheese!"

Getting to his feet, the headstander failed in his attempt at a flashy no-hand's maneuver and collapsed, to widespread laughter. Mr. Shy, in perfect dignity, continued to dine.

In a moment or two, a speaker got to his feet.

"Ladies and gentlemen," he began. "You all know the cause which has gathered us here tonight, to raise money to help the little feller in whom our teacher has taken so much interest. Margaret, won't you say a few words now? We all want to say what a wonderful job with this little boy we think you've done."

Margaret shook her head. Lewis, the little boy who had cut in on the dancers, was eating his supper, unaware what was going on. But everyone else knew. And they smiled on him with a certain newly developing pity.

The story went back to the beginning of the school year, to the family with three children who supplied one-third of Margaret's enrollment. They were an underprivileged family, fatherless, the mother working hard for a strange and little-known man who dwelt across the river. Lewis was ten years old, the middle child of the three; his older brother, a sharply intelligent sixth grader; his little sister in the second grade. By rights Lewis should have been in the fourth grade. But somewhere along the line something had gone wrong. The soft spot in a baby's head, which closes so soon after birth, had never closed for Lewis. A blow on the head could have killed him at any time in the past ten years, but he had lived and grown somewhat normally to the average physical stature of a ten-year old. It was only in Lewis's eyes and the expression of his face that you could see something was missing. He could understand what was said to him; he could answer in a slow and hesitant way. But he was definitely mentally deficient, and he had never been to school. The teachers hadn't wanted him. So for ten years he had languished around the edges of a poverty-stricken family, ignored by a mother whose chief concern lay in keeping herself and the others somehow alive, teased and tormented by his brother and sister who had never been taught other ways of behaving, and made dimly, painfully aware that he was not like other people, not good enough to go to school.

Miss Miller heard about him when she accepted the teaching position at the Garland School. She decided at once to include him. He came on the first day, frightened and pitifully hopeful, legs shaking in tattered overalls, overcome by the fact that this person with laughing eyes and curly black hair treated him like the other kids and was glad to see him.

Patiently, slowly, she had worked with him all year, buying with her own money specially simple books for him to use, sitting up at night coloring pictures to teach him the meanings of up and down, in and out; thrilling when, after months and months, he finally learned to count to five. For her, Lewis presented a fascinating educational challenge. For him, this teacher was life itself. He had never known such goodness before.

But his progress in learning was painfully slow. After a year at the Garland School, and after much consultation with the county nurse, it appeared that there was one hope for Lewis—an examination and diagnosis by specialists who lived hundreds of miles away. His mother had fought all such proposals before. Would she now allow him to go? And if so, from what source could the money for traveling come?

There are ways of getting things done in small communities even under the doubtful leadership of a teacher. One was my way. If you wanted the schoolroom painted, go ahead and paint it. Don't ask for advice or help. And you will work against the resistance of everybody in the community. The other way, Margaret Miller's way, was far more subtle. She wanted to get Lewis to that doctor. So she dropped a few words to a few people—and let the community take it from there.

The plan worked partly because of the generosity of this particular community and in part because of the method Margaret used. But anyway, here we all were, cheering and raising money to send Lewis to the doctor. Mrs. Jackson, the school board leader, had decided to visit her friends who lived near the doctors, taking Margaret and the boy along with her. And money was collected from all to pay for his other expenses. The mother miraculously assented and signed permission for him to go. Before leaving, he spent several nights in the schoolhouse, following Miss Miller around like a little dog—learning to be away from home.

And she denied having had anything to do with the matter. The community had thought of it, she insisted; theirs was the credit.

In return for her generous, unselfish leadership, the community would have done anything on earth for her. She and Lewis departed for the doctor with the blessings of all who had helped them.

﹖

Margaret and I enjoyed some fun times together, and the Friday overnights I spent at her teacherage remain especially vivid in memory. We ventured forth to visit neighbors on many a spring evening, learning much about the country and its people. There was a visit to the unbeatable Sam Shy and his wife, who dwelt miles up a gumbo road extending up-country from the graveled arterial route that pulsed bumpily to Miles City.

Mr. Shy and his wife, also named Margaret, had lived and worked by themselves on their rolling little ranch for many years. It held an air of ancient prairie—richly grassed, alive with golden antelope that whistled and sprang from their resting places to gallop over the nearest hill, white rumps flashing in the sun. So much open space uncrossed by fence or road, house or tree, mottled with the drifting shadows of cloud and sun, was a breath of heaven. And their cattle always brought a gasp from spectators at the sale ring in town, where small, one- or two-year-old animals of regular coloring are the everyday rule. Perhaps it was impractical or unwise to raise them in this manner, but the Sam Shy cattle were not small nor regular in any sense. They included magnificent five- and six-year-old steers, gigantic in size, ranging from whiteface to roan to solid mahogany red, with horns reaching from their heads into rare majestic crowns. It is simply not done anymore to leave horns on cattle, nor to let steers grow out to full, almost horse-high size. Baby beef and dehorned heads that will not poke a fellow's tenderloin on route to market—these are what the public wants. Sam

Shy was gloriously uninterested in what the public wanted. He cross-bred Durham bulls into his big Herefords for the sheer size and weight they imparted, and to hell with the public. As for the horns—God gave them horns, didn't He? Did He figure on men chopping them off again?

The Shys' life must have been a lonely one during their years of working together outside and in. Margaret Shy had had horses fall on her, and had lost her temper once and kicked a tractor tire, breaking her toe. Yet their house, polished and immaculate, welcomed one with an easy graciousness. Their hospitality was boundless, their store of tales inexhaustible. On the evening Margaret and I invaded them, we stayed the night. Sam, exploding before we went to bed, said, "There's too damn many Margarets and Margots around here! From now on, my wife is Margaret. And you—Miss Miller—are 'Get'! And Pringle is 'Go'!"

We two teachers, "Get" and "Go," remained until the end of the school year.

We visited, soon afterward, Tom Gilmore, whose recitations of poems of the olden days had been featured at so many an intermission at the schoolhouse dances.

We also visited, on a final evening, a newer arrival to the country, whose tragic story reflected a number of truths about the broader Montana way of life. Tommy Furness lived alone in a beautiful old house built by a Scotchman on his own land who had cowboyed his way through life in the general area of Tongue River. Unmarried, the Scotchman—who still cherished a silver sword from his father's noble family at home—had no one in mind to succeed him on the Tongue River ranch built through a life's work. Then Ben Furness, Tommy's brother, had drifted in from the East and taken a job there. Everyone liked Ben. Tall, good-looking, cheerful—he learned well. For an easterner he took fast to the ranching life, and the ranching people to him. The Scotchman left the ranch to him.

Months later, driving a truck into a granary, Ben Furness was killed. Tommy had been working near his brother when it happened. Through the whole horrible business it began to appear that the ranch would go to him. Younger than Ben, shyer, more of a dreamer, Tommy stayed on alone in the massive house, which leaned out, on stilts almost, over the river—closing him off, as it did the SH people farther south, from the rest of the neighborhood.

Tommy was courteous, attractive, but seemingly hard to know. We had visited other people, Margaret and I reasoned. Why not Tommy? He had begged us to come!

We set off for his place, parking the car at the riverbank across from his house. Here the river was far too deep to ford. There was no bridge, no go-devil. But there was a rowboat, lying innocently upside down on our bank.

"I'll wade over and get you!" shouted Tommy from the other side. "Stay there!"

We considered. Were we such helpless creatures as all that? Was there no character or independence in modern womanhood? Had I not, after all, paddled many a canoe on placid eastern waters? Margaret was dubious, being from North Dakota, where water is generally not plentiful enough for paddling. But she was game, as usual.

While Tommy rushed into the house for his wading boots, we got the boat right-side up and into the water. Margaret clenched rather greenly at her oar as we shoved off. For a moment all was well.

"Now, pull!" I directed. Both oars dipped and then shot above the surface, flinging a sprinkle of cold drops. Not deep enough. "Pull again!" This time we failed to synchronize, and the boat wafted uncertainly into the current. "Pull!"

The boat, taking matters over, did not wish to be pulled—at least not by us. Its bow described three circles, corkscrewing us faster and faster into the mid-river current. Rowing madly, we could get only brief glimpses of the shoreline, which seemed to be gliding smoothly past us as the boat revolved slowly downstream. There was not any stopping the boat, though we could reach the gravelly bottom with the oars. Round and round she went, farther and farther downstream. Where was the house? Where was Tommy?

Tommy, heroically, was trying to catch up with us by running along the brushy banks and shouting directions we could not hear. A muffled splashing, a looming figure, and a sudden lurch were the first news we had of him as, long-legging it into the riverbed, he overtook the bow of the boat and seized its dangling mooring rope.

We had traveled half a mile in a very few minutes. Little was said as Tommy, splashing and panting, hauled us all the way back up the river, in the boat, to his house. His reflections during that laborious twenty minutes were never disclosed. But, once on terra firma, everyone had a good time. We talked and laughed, and made a pan of the most inedible candy. When we returned across the river, Tommy rowed us there—with no objections from us at all.

It was only a few months later when, galloping home at dusk one evening, Tommy's horse fell with him in such a manner that he lay unconscious for many hours before being found. Suffering from paralysis, he never fully recovered. It seems ironic that such accidents should have happened twice to men so new to the country. Goodness knows they happened often enough to longtime residents over a period of years.

There was John, a rancher popular with all, who had been riding after a bunch of horses down a creek one evening, pretty fast in order to keep up with them. His horse stepped on a rock, somersaulted, and fell, leaving him unconscious, with a broken back. He lay there, unable to move, for two days and nights before he was finally found.

"Don't move me," he whispered when his rescuers approached, "or you'll damn sure kill me. Go down and take that door off the hinges at the school. You can carry me on that."

They did as he told them, hurrying down to Garland where they unhinged the schoolhouse door for use as a stretcher.

They got him home all right, but a week or two later, John died.

Such stories are not totally disconnected from the reasons why cowboys—the real ones—are the way they are. The real ones are not common any longer, and among prospectors and buffalo skinners, soldiers and speculators and homesteaders, they never were. Each generation of cowboys considers itself the last. But each drills its passions so thoroughly into its children that the generations inevitably go on. And there is a conscious disregard of danger. When you are born on a horse, asking is not good enough; when you have circled freely after cattle, or outrun a bunch of wild horses many miles down some rocky ridge, no other work can ever be the same. Because there is a fierce pride in the cowboy art, and its practitioners are artists—temperamental, prejudiced, quietly convinced of their superiority to other human beings, they are not easy to know. They do not give themselves freely to strangers. And many a sophisticated critic has gone away convinced that the blunt-toed farm hands on Main Street are all that exist. Sophisticates have lacked the eyes and souls to see.

There's a bit of magic in it, like seeing the "little people" in an older country. The little people show themselves rarely and to true sympathizers alone. Otherwise, they don't go to the trouble.

You've got to believe. You've got to know some of the language. And among dude ranch patrons, musicians, farmers, and fakes well-clothed in imitation, you've got to know where to look. You may not care to take the trouble. But if you do, you will find the old silver-spurred profession, changed not too much from the books you read as a kid, running like a golden thread through the urban and suburban and farming populations of any western town.

CHAPTER NINE

Continuing Education,
and Teacher, Goodbye

As I later reconstructed the scene, a lean, bespectacled professor stood at the front of a classroom in one of Miles City's elementary schools, selecting from a sea of waving hands in front of him.

"All right, Mrs. McCrae. What do you think was the author's purpose?"

Mrs. McCrae, a tiny lady in her fifties, stood up. "Well if you ask me, the fellow who wrote that story just didn't know very much," she announced. "Seems to me like no normal people on earth would have acted like they did, that girl getting crowned and all. I mean, it just doesn't seem *real*."

Uncalled on, another lady stood up. "Yes, I believe they might have been just like that," she replied. "A lot of city people and especially newspaper reporters act pretty strange. You can't tell *what* they're going to do. When I lived in Seattle, there was one of those reporters hanging around the morgue all the time."

"That's because of their nose for news," commented a third lady. "Looks to me like a nose for none of their damned business."

"Order, please," rapped the professor. "Now what we are trying to find out is, just what was the author trying to say? Was he just telling us a story? Or was there a deeper meaning behind the story for us to understand? Yes, Mrs. Jones?"

"He was trying to show how those colleges can be hard on people, maybe," commented Mrs. Jones. "I mean, that poor girl working so hard and all to please her folks and all the time she had a bad heart."

"Why do you suppose she thought she had to work so hard?" queried the professor. "Was it the college's fault, or society's?"

Bewilderment crept over several faces, as the audience members waited for enlightenment. Having just read a short story by one of America's more cynical modern writers, Sherman Anderson, they had missed some of his withering attacks on a high-powered, dehumanized world. Rural Montana was still fairly human by comparison. And this gathering was composed, strictly, of Montana teachers—most of them from country schools—who were augmenting their college credits by taking a Saturday extension course on the Modern Short Story.

The extension courses, given through the State Teachers College, were one way Montana had tackled its goal of licking the teacher shortage. Due to the lack of qualified candidates, the state was forced to hire many underqualified people each year, issuing them temporary certificates, which could be renewed year after year, so long as they went to school and earned twelve more credits each per year. Many did this work during college summer sessions. Many others were able to avoid the travel and board expense of that system by loading up on correspondence and extension courses at home.

The teachers continued to wrangle over Anderson's hidden intentions until one o'clock, at which precise moment they bade him farewell and rushed in a body to Main Street and the local cafés. They had exactly thirty minutes to eat lunch and then hoof it over to the high school for the second extension course of the day—dealing with local nature study.

Somewhat breathless, the crowd for the second course assembled. It contained most of the short-story people, and a few new additions like myself—who did not need the other particular type of course credit. Two such courses were offered each fall and spring, totaling ten to twelve available credits. One could take what one wanted; there were no obligations. The nature study course, employing a local teacher, was cheaper. For the short story class, the ladies had to pay the bus fare of a professor who journeyed from Billings weekly. Both were offered as part of the spring session.

The local teacher, Mr. Hanna, stocky and pleasant-faced, addressed the gathering at precisely 1:30. "As you know, ladies," he began, "today we will have one of our little hikes. You have all signed up for cars to travel in; now, is anyone lacking transportation?"

Apparently no one was. Teachers with cars were transporting other teachers with no cars, sometimes even putting the touch on them for twenty-five cents gas money. After a few more instructions, young and old, we loaded up. The instructor's maroon Ford led our cavalcade several miles up the highway into a stretch of high, rolling pine hills, where we parked and got out.

Mr. Hanna addressed us, thirty in number, a strange gleam in his eye—like that of a sailor newly returned to his favorite sea.

"Now, just come along with me," he instructed, "and if you have any questions, let me know." He streaked off at a pace that was almost a dog-trot, and we strung out behind him.

"What are we s'posed to be hunting for today?" puffed an elderly woman at my side. "Rocks or cactuses or what?"

"Wild flowers, I think," was my answer. And sure enough, ahead of us was forming a little knot of teachers around small specimens of flora, over which Mr. Hanna was standing paternally.

"Now this," he informed us, "is a Butte Candle, one of the flowers that Mrs. Custer mentioned in her book on the western prairies."

"Did Custer come through here?" someone asked.

"No," replied Mr. Hanna. "But he did follow across that ridge over there. They say the Indians laid a trail ahead of him, with lots of horses, to get him to pass by one of the alkali springs over there. It was a hot day and the soldiers were terribly thirsty, so they all tanked up on that alkali water. It made them so sick they could hardly fight, that day of the massacre."

"Well my great uncle said it was liquor," announced a teacher in the rear ranks. "He said Custer and those men cached a whole bunch of whiskey down by the old mouth of Tongue River when they camped one night, and if you knew where to look you could probably still dig it up!" (The accounts suggested here were not actually true.)

We departed from the Butte Candle, ruminating on the fate of Custer. And so the afternoon went, with goatlike scrambles up and down the gravelly hills, and many a stocking snagged on sheep scale or greasewood. From Mr. Hanna, to relay to our children, we received mimeographed outlines on local natural history, ranging from geology to the love life of the cottonwood tree. I attempted to relay the latter, some days later, to Gene in his science period.

"Aw, come on, Miss Margot!" he cackled. "Who fed you that?"

But it was all in the line of self-improvement, and we takers of the courses were most grateful for the opportunity.

On the way home, lurching through ruts and standing water, it dawned on me that the school year had nearly ended.

For a child, the close of school brings forth few feelings other than sheer, unbridled joy. The summer seems to stretch ahead in a golden chain of deliriously free days to play, to go fishing, to travel toward new horizons in the family car. No more lessons, no more books, no more teacher's dirty looks—or, as we used to carol so merrily, "Hark the herald angels shout! No more days till we get out! No more days till we are free, from this place of misery!"

As a teacher, one's sensations are slightly different. The last month or two may have been a grind, the last weeks and days of school counted impatiently. But come the last day or two, one's mood changes.

I began watching the SH youngsters nostalgically at recess, savoring the last hours, wanting to remember all of this and keep it in my memory forever: our classroom; the first-grade club, with its piled orange-crate shelves and fairy ring of cottonwood stump "toad stools"; the science table now emptied of its mouse and its February gardens and the goldfish who had frozen to death; the stove now cold with disuse; the walls painted so laboriously; and the frieze of Indian pictures hung with pride above the green blackboards. How much had gone into this, now nearly over.

The kids were happily at play in the May sunshine. Dick, no longer the bundle of nerves who came to school in the fall, was now good-humored and sure of himself, not so quick to thump his fists on the table in defiance with the cry "I can't! I just can't!" He still wagged his head and told his wild tales, but there was now about him a certain new air of assurance. Only that morning he had he told me proudly, "Well, Miss Margot, when I get to that new school, you know what I'm gonna do? I'm gonna take my cap off and say good morning to the teacher, first thing!"

Eddie was now brimming with confidence—as the best reader in the first grade. And Leslie, slower at school work but triumphant as a leader of the small fry, was a changed boy from the one who had been so sadly lost the first few days. He had said back then, when the others were stating favorite kinds of schoolwork, "I don't know. I'd ruther do nothing. I'd ruther just sit." And now, it was Leslie, with an air of authority, speaking for the rest of them: "Teacher, we want to go up across into them hills and look for some wild flowers. Okay, Teacher?"

Gary—forever Gary—was the only one who would not pass the first grade. I had conferred with his mother, and our decision was more or less mutual—that Gary, the following year, would be better off as an advanced first-grader than as a handicapped second-grader. There was not one slow fiber in Gary's mind, and we felt it would be a shame to discourage him by requiring work he was not ready to do. He had done amazingly well for a five-year-old and was loved by all as an unfailing source of comic relief. Days before, he had entered the school flushed with excitement, yellow hair rumpled as he jerked his cap off. "Ole sow at Miller's just had she pigs," he announced breathlessly, "and she had a whole bunch of 'em, eleven, and Aunt Betty says she only got dinner plates for eight!"

We had all laughed at his concern and soon learned that Betty was feeding the three extra piglets with an eyedropper.

And then there was Pansy—our perfect lady. I had always felt as if Pansy had been transposed somehow from a setting that would have suited her better, some expensive school in the East for refined and wealthy little girls. She would have fitted there perfectly. Here, she had her troubles. Brilliant in school work, she had to fight for her rights as the only girl in a boy's world. They had ceded to her, little by little, as time went by. She could run pretty fast in playground games and kick pretty hard when they roped her, for all her fresh face and shining curls. And she could still beat up her brother Leslie when she had to, even if he was leader of the first grade.

Gene was not of a mind to stick with school much longer, and I wondered if he would even stay on for the eighth grade next year. He wanted to be a man good and fast, leading a man's life, working for wages, driving too fast in a borrowed car till he could manage to buy his own. School had given him, over the past years, as much learning as his people would ever demand of him, as much as his life would ever call for. Be thankful, I told myself, that he had made some progress and had some fun—and that now we were parting pretty good friends.

And Billy—well, Billy had come farther than any of them. It was hard to associate this eager kid with the boy he had once been. There was the way he had stared into thin air, refusing to see or hear me, and the bitter hardening of his eyes under criticism or correction. Not that he was over it; he still snarled at the stepmother who did her utmost to care for him; he was still guarded and hostile, at times toward teacher and schoolmates, among whom he was fighting hard for recognition—something important to a child who has never had it. But the recognition was being gained, little by little, as he learned to play fair instead of cheating or bullying on our playground; and he began to carry better and better report cards home to the parents who read them with so appraising an eye. The report cards had been designed with some care, in fact, knowing that Eddie's straight A's as a snappy first-grader would throw a shadow of painful comparison over the older Billy.

And yet there was no sense giving the rascal better than he deserved—especially considering those first few painful weeks, when a smile or half-agreeable assent out of Billy represented a battle hard-won against big odds. There were times when a person wanted to smash him to pieces for his insolent "Go-to-hell!" attitude, which he managed to convey in every movement and every line of his carefully expressionless face. On the first report I had written—after great deliberation—a comment that had hurt him pretty badly, for all the forbearance I used in constructing what I thought was a pretty mild statement of facts. During the next few weeks I redoubled my efforts to reach him. Thanking God for a new beginning, I wrote better things the second time and sent it home, knowing he would fare a little better with his parents.

And he did not let me down, which made me feel perhaps more strongly than a teacher should, that here was a child to fight for as hard as possible and to believe in with all one's heart.

Because many children in this world have few real friends. If they can count their parents among those who look on them with compassion, they are fortunate. Yet sometimes compassion is best tempered with a depth of understanding hard to come by, although terribly significant—and the child who cannot find it at home may turn to another grown person a time or two, a teacher or someone else. If the grown-ups fail him, his world offers little but the violent alternatives that so many children have tragically chosen. O parents, O teachers the world over, when will you truly learn?

Once sensing this, I found there is yet a lesson to be learned by those who want to help and who think they understand. As if by magic, one may watch a bit of frozen and frightened humanity warming into life and beginning to grow, not because you have done it yourself but simply because you have cleared the air a little while, giving some protection from shock, if only enough to let the process begin. For others it is often hard to see: that barren spot in a field, surrounded by growing plants—surely that spot is barren, retarded, unproductive within the whole greening context of other acres. Only the person who has worked in it can see the change begun in this barren place, can have faith and believe that this place nurtured with some special care may bear good fruit in its season.

And that is the case of the slow children, the hurt and crippled ones who heal so painfully and advance with such little steps. If only one could keep them at school under one's wing a year or two, and be sure that the advance would not be halted in infancy by yet another bitter wind!

But it cannot be done, except in rare cases. It could not be done in mine. And when I left Billy, I knew—and it was a bitter knowledge— that his new teacher would never pamper him as I had, nor find him story horses to play with, nor create stories of Billy himself on a wild Brahma bull. That is your final test as a teacher, perhaps. You must ask yourself, in full awareness, whether you can let them go, knowing your little time has left them so badly prepared against the times to come, knowing you have given them so precious little armor against the things they shall be dealt. It is a knowledge that is sometimes very hard to swallow with the children you have felt most about, and worked hardest with, and who have affected you more deeply than should be allowed. You know you must not allow yourself to go overboard, nor be torn too badly by the knowledge that this work, this time, may have been in vain. Fate in a way has ordained the lives of children, and it can be changed by a teacher only along a narrow, brief margin. It is reminiscent of the wonderful, honest doctor who first admitted that, of the sick, a number will get well, but a number will die—whether or not he ever treats them. Only a narrow few may be saved or damned by what he does for them. Likewise, a teacher must realize the fields that are closed to her, the children foredoomed, and not waste strength in regrets and bitterness on the cases, however touching, that despite all efforts may fail.

Otherwise you can go crazy, fighting all of life and its dictum that this one shall be handicapped, this one unblemished and strong. The balance of fate can by swayed, but only slightly, and to keep on year after year at swaying it where possible, you must not allow the major unalterable injustices to tear too fiercely at your heart.

Yes, summer was a-coming in, with its veil of green brightening along the river cottonwoods, the new emerald alfalfa, the geese returning north.

On the last day of school, we worked on our exhibit for the fair, then had ice cream before the children all went home. There was no pausing for goodbyes or farewell speeches when school was out. They pelted out the door full tilt.

All my things were packed and gone, the schoolroom stripped to its essentials, the teacherage bare of anything that had been mine. I had no reason to remain. It was back to its beginnings, the same place I had entered with such misgivings in the fall. It was hard for me to believe how quickly it had become home—and hard to realize that I was really leaving. The whole building echoed to my tread. Annie, saddled and tied to the fence outside, shifted restlessly. Under the wind, the windmill screeched in its rusty voice. Then all was still.

As I left, I looked the embroidered Indian on my rocking chair squarely in the eye. "With Pipe of Peace All Troubles Cease," reminded the raveled motto.

Quickly I shut the door and untied Annie, leading her, for the last time, out the barbed-wire gate. The wind sang in my ears as we thundered at full speed down the twisting mile to the Hirsches'—past the Hirsch kids and Gene, who were shooting homemade bows and arrows, inspired by our Indian unit.

"Don't take any wooden nickels," shouted Gene, as we slowed to go through the gate.

And they were gone.

Epilogue

"Twilight" and "Nocturne"

Twilight

Early Spring, 1954

Six o'clock now and still
Light round the western sky,
Rose blending blue

Winter is leaving us
Minutes each day
Of later sunset, earlier dawn
And puffs of low, smoke cloud

A handful of steady stars
And a low crystalline moon
A pup chasing his tail in the dark
And hoofbeats drumbeats on the shed floor sounding.

This is the end of my day—
With the light pole humming its six wires
And the cottonwood reaching long arms
Past the motionless windmill
Into the evening sky.

Nocturne

SH School, 1954

Gazing at the sky tonight,
Harkening to evening bells
Of milk cows, where a spark of light
Marks the place my neighbor dwells

Reaching south and stretching north,
Long and low the sunset lies,
Sending glowing streamers forth
Half the circle of the skies.

Postscript

After leaving the SH School in the spring of 1954, Margot Liberty taught for four years among the Northern Cheyenne of Montana at the Birney Day School sixty miles farther north along Tongue River. In 1958 she worked with John Stands In Timber on their coauthored book *Cheyenne Memories*. Her daughter, Paula, was born in 1959 and her son, Henry, in 1961.

Margot taught a fifth-grade class in Sheridan, Wyoming, at the Woodland Park School in 1962 and 1963, and served as a Ranger Historian at Custer Battlefield National Monument (now Little Bighorn Battlefield National Monument) during those summers. She then went on to the University of Minnesota to earn a doctorate in anthropology, completed after five years of study, after which she became a faculty member successively at the Universities of Nebraska, Missouri, and Pittsburgh.

Margot moved to Sheridan, Wyoming, serving as director of the Trail End Historic Site for the Wyoming State Parks twelve years prior to her retirement.

She has written six books and more than thirty professional articles in Plains Indian anthropology and history. A complete record of her research and publications through 2010 can be found in the "Bibliography of scholarship" on pages 285–314 of her book of poetry, *Songs and Snippets: Poems by Margot Liberty*.

She continues to live in Sheridan, Wyoming.

Notes

Preface

1. My father, Henry F. Pringle, won the Pulitzer Prize for his biography of Theodore Roosevelt in 1931 (*Theodore Roosevelt: A Biography* [Orlando; Harcourt]). He was an important figure in Franklin D. Roosevelt's Office of War Information during World War II. My mother, Helena Huntington Smith, wrote three classic works of western American history, including *We Pointed Them North*, with E. C. (Teddy Blue) Abbott (1939); *A Bride Goes West*, with Nanny Tiffany Alderson (1941); and *The War on Powder River* (1962). As historian Arthur M. Schlesinger, Jr., noted, "Larry McMurtry considers *We Pointed Them North* the best single memoir of the cowboy era." Of my father, Schlesinger said, "[When] I began the search for a job in Washington [in 1942], [Archibald] MacLeish sent me to Henry F. Pringle, chief of the Writers Bureau of the Office of War Information . . . I knew of Pringle by reputation. . . . A journalist in the twenties, his biography of Theodore Roosevelt, published in 1931, was a brilliant, witty, skeptical account based on thorough and careful research. It won the Pulitzer Prize of 1931 and set the tone of commentary on TR for a generation or two. . . . The Writers Division was an unusually cohesive group with uncommonly high esprit de corps. Henry Pringle was a father figure for the younger people. He was wise, wry, considerate, protective, with the uncommon gift of phrasing criticism in the most courtly and acceptable way." Of my mother, Schlesinger said: "Henry Pringle was married to Helena Huntington Smith, an attractive, intelligent, competitive and sometimes devastatingly frank woman." Arthur M. Schlesinger, Jr., *A Life in the Twentieth Century: Innocent Beginnings*, vol. 1, 1917–1950 (Boston: Houghton Mifflin, 2000), 264–65, 280, 287.

2. John Stands in Timber and Margot Liberty, *Cheyenne Memories* (New Haven: Yale University Press, 1967), with a second edition in 1998 and translations into Italian and French.

3. The first conference, in 1976, was "American Indian Intellectuals," U.S. Centennial Conference of the American Ethnological Society, Atlanta. Its proceedings were published in 1978 as *American Indian Intellectuals, Proceedings of the American Ethnological Society* (St. Paul, Minn.: West Publishing), and reissued (without illustrations) in 2002 as *American Indian Intellectuals of the Nineteenth and Early Twentieth Centuries* (Norman: University of Oklahoma Press). The second conference, also in 1976, and organized with W. Raymond Wood, was "Anthropology on the Great Plains," 34th Plains Conference Centennial Symposium, Minneapolis. Its proceedings were published in 1980 as *Anthropology on the Great Plains* (Lincoln: University of Nebraska Press). My article "Cheyenne Primacy: New Perspectives on a Great Plains Tribe," with W. Raymond Wood, *Plains Anthropologist* 56, no. 218 (May 2011), 155–82, contains the most complete summary of my work and conclusions concerning Northern Cheyenne ethnohistory. A self-published book of poetry, *Songs and Snippets: Poems by Margot Liberty* (n.p., ExLibris, 2010), contains in addition to 339 poems a complete bibliography of more than one hundred items of my research and scholarship through 2010.

Prologue

1. Of the schools mentioned in this book, several were still functioning in 1984 according to the book *America's Country Schools* by Andrew Gulliford (Washington, D.C.: National Trust for Historic Preservation, 1984), 271. I have not been able to ascertain whether these schools are continuing as of 2016.

Further Readings

Bial, Raymond. *One-Room School*. New York: Houghton Mifflin Harcourt, 1999.

Caldwell, Charlotte. *Visions and Voices: Montana's One-Room Schoolhouses*. With a foreword by Ivan Doig. Clyde Park, Mont.: Barn Board Press, 2012.

Gordon, Julia Weber. *My Country School Diary: An Adventure in Creative Teaching*. New York: Harper and Brothers, 1946.

Gulliford, Andrew. *America's Country Schools*. With a note from Barbara Bush. Washington, D.C.: Preservation Press, 1991.

Kauffman, Henry J. *The American One-Room Schoolhouse*. Morgantown, Pa.: Masthof Press, 1997.

Rocheleau, Paul. *The One-Room Schoolhouse: A Tribute to a Beloved National Icon*. New York: Universe Publishing, 2003.

CPSIA information can be obtained
at www.ICGtesting.com
Printed in the USA
LVHW010623020622
720217LV00003B/348

9 780806 190020